FORMER SOVIET REPUBLICS

KAZAKHSTAN

KYRGYZSTAN

THE CENTRAL ASIAN STATES

BY CHERESE CARTLIDGE
AND CHARLES CLARK

TAJIKISTAN

TURKMENISTAN

UZBEKISTAN

LUCENT BOOKS
P.O. BOX 289011
SAN DIEGO, CA 92198-9011

Library of Congress Cataloging-in-Publication Data

Cartlidge, Cherese.
  The Central Asian states / by Cherese Cartlidge & Charles Clark
    p.   cm. — (Modern nations of the world)
  Includes bibliographical references and index.
  ISBN 1-56006-735–7 (alk. paper)
  1. Asia, Central—Juvenile literature.   [1. Asia, Central.]   I. Clark,
Charles, 1949– II. Title.   III. Series.
  DK851 .C37 2001
  958—dc21   00-011526

Copyright © 2001 by Lucent Books, Inc.
P.O. Box 289011, San Diego, CA 92198-9011
Printed in the U.S.A.

CONTENTS

FOREWORD   4
  The Curtain Rises

INTRODUCTION   7
  The Silk Road in the Twenty-First Century

CHAPTER ONE   10
  The Land and People

CHAPTER TWO   26
  From the Silk Road to the
  Fall of the Soviet Union

CHAPTER THREE   40
  The Independent States of Central Asia

CHAPTER FOUR   56
  Daily Life in Central Asia

CHAPTER FIVE   77
  A Rich Cultural Tapestry

CHAPTER SIX   89
  Conflict and Cooperation Along
  the New Silk Road

  Facts About the Central Asian States   107
  Notes   111
  Chronology   114
  Suggestions for Further Reading   118
  Works Consulted   120
  Index   123
  Picture Credits   128
  About the Authors   128

FOREWORD

THE CURTAIN RISES

Through most of the last century, the world was widely perceived as divided into two realms separated by what British prime minister Winston Churchill once called the "iron curtain." This curtain was, of course, not really made of iron, but of ideas and values. Countries to the west of this symbolic curtain, including the United States, were democracies founded upon the economic principles of capitalism. To the east, in the Soviet Union, a new social and economic order known as communism prevailed. The United States and the Soviet Union were locked for much of the twentieth century in a struggle for military, economic, and political dominance around the world.

But the Soviet Union could not sustain its own weight, burdened as it was by a hugely inefficient centralized government bureaucracy, by long-term neglect of domestic needs in favor of spending untold billions on the military, and by the systematic repression of thought and expression among its citizens. For years the military and internal police apparatus had held together the Soviet Union's diverse peoples. But even these entities could not overcome the corruption, the inefficiency, and the inability of the Communist system to provide the basic necessities for the Soviet people.

The unrest that signaled the beginning of the end for the Soviet Union began in the satellite countries of Eastern Europe in 1988—in East Germany, followed by Hungary, and Poland. By 1990, the independence movement had moved closer to the Soviet heartland. Lithuania became the first Baltic nation to declare its independence. By December 1991, all fifteen union republics— Armenia, Azerbaijan, Belarus, Estonia, Georgia, Kazakhstan, Kyrgyzstan, Latvia, Lithuania, Moldova, Russia, Tajikistan, Turkmenistan, Ukraine, Uzbekistan—had done the same. The Soviet Union had officially ceased to exist.

Today the people of new nations such as Uzbekistan, Latvia, Belarus, Georgia, Ukraine, and Russia itself (still the largest nation on earth) must deal with the loss of the certainties of the Soviet era and face the new economic and social challenges of the present. The fact that many of these regions have little if any history of self-governance adds to the problem. For better or worse, many social problems were kept in check by a powerful government during the Soviet era, and long-standing cultural, ethnic, and other tensions are once again threatening to tear apart these new and fragile nations. Whether these regions make an effective transition to a market economy based on capitalism and resolve their internal economic crises by becoming vital and successful participants in world trade; whether their social crises push them back in the direction of dictatorship or civil war, or move them toward greater political, ethnic, and religious tolerance; and perhaps most important of all, whether average citizens can come to believe in their own ability to improve their lives and their own power to create a government and a nation of laws that works in their own best

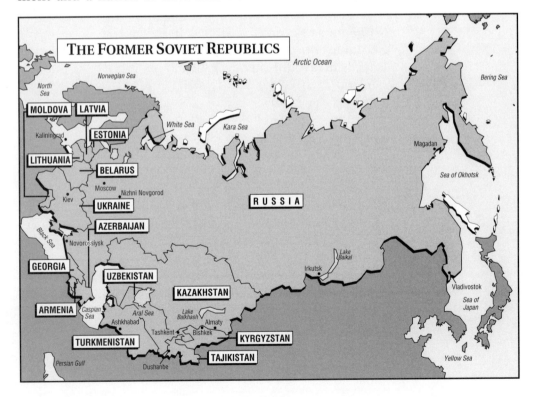

interests, are questions that the entire world, not just former Soviet citizens are pondering.

Sociologists and political scientists alike point to instability in the former Soviet republics as a serious threat to world peace and the balance of global power, and therefore it is more important than ever to be accurately informed about this politically and economically critical part of the world. With Modern Nations: Former Soviet Republics, Lucent Books provides information about the people and recent history of the former Soviet republics, with an emphasis on those aspects of their culture, history, and current situation that seem most likely to play a role in the future course of each of these new nations emerging from the shadows of the now vanished iron curtain.

INTRODUCTION
THE SILK ROAD IN THE TWENTY-FIRST CENTURY

Central Asia is a region both united by commonalities and divided by diversity. The peoples of Central Asia have many different cultural heritages. Their ancestors came from many lands—China, Mongolia, India, Greece, Persia, and Russia, to name just a few. Yet they also share common traditions that have grown out of the region's role as the principal land route between Europe and China, known as the Silk Road. Most of the people of Central Asia are Muslim, but there are significant minorities of all the other major world religions. Many of their languages are related, deriving from Turkic, and after a century and a half of Russian and Soviet colonialism, many people also speak Russian. Now, as the Central Asian States enter the world stage as independent nations, some even suggest that English, the language of business in the developed world, should become the common second language of Central Asia.

The people of Central Asia are proud of their newly independent countries, but they still need help from the developed nations. They want to retain their ancient traditions yet participate in the modern world. Their strategic location, rich history, vast natural resources, well-educated populace, and long experience as traders and entrepreneurs mean that the Central Asian States will likely be one of the most exciting and dynamic regions of the world in the coming decades.

But despite all the potential for economic and cultural development in Central Asia, there are many divisions and conflicts in the region. The history of war among the peoples of the region and with invaders is long and complex. The major ethnic groups—the Kazakhs, Kyrgyz, Tajiks, Turkmen, and Uzbeks—have been the source of the national identities of the republics in the Soviet era and since independence. However, each of the Central Asian States has sizable minorities who sometimes want to retain their ethnic identities and control their local governments. For example, a large part of Uzbekistan is the Karakalpak Autonomous Republic, where

THE CENTRAL ASIAN STATES

RUSSIA

RUSSIA

KAZAKHSTAN

⊛ Astana

Aral Sea

Syr Darya River

Lake Balkhash

Caspian Sea

UZBEKISTAN

Bishkek
⊛

TURKMENISTAN

Tashkent
⊛

KYRGYZSTAN

CHINA

Amu Darya River

Ashkhabad
⊛

Dushanbe
⊛

TAJIKISTAN

⊛ Capital city

AZERBAIJAN

IRAN

AFGHANISTAN

PAKISTAN

INDIA

the majority of the people are of the Karakalpak ethnic group; this arrangement was begun in the 1920s to avoid conflicts between Karakalpaks and Uzbeks. In Western countries like the United States, people of many ethnic backgrounds can be brought into the mainstream of life because they have access to economic and political participation. In Central Asia, however, it is more difficult for ethnic groups to find common ground. For example, some groups live as sedentary farmers while others are nomadic herders, and the two lifestyles often do not mix easily.

A HISTORY OF CULTURAL DIVERSITY

The Central Asian States are the product of a variety of historical influences, including commerce and conquest. The region lies at the heart of the Silk Road, the system of overland trade routes between China and Europe. Rather than a single caravan route, as the name implies, the Silk Road was a network that developed over many centuries. Silk, one of the earliest items to be traded, gave the road its name and has been carried through this region from China since ancient times. With the importance of trade came an eagerness for various rulers to control the region. Beginning with

Alexander the Great, Central Asia has been conquered many times, by the Mongols, the Persians, the Arabs, and others. Although these conquests brought misery and destruction for the native peoples of the region, they also brought new languages, religions, crafts, and technologies.

In the nineteenth century, the last major powers to vie for the region squared off. Britain was expanding its control over India, to the southeast of Central Asia, and the Russian Empire was both jealous and frightened at the prospect of a major Western military power with that sort of global reach. Thus began what has become known as the Great Game, the political, diplomatic, and sometimes military battle between Russia and Britain for control of Central Asia. The Russian Empire won the Great Game but lost the battle for its own survival in the Communist Revolution of 1917. The new Soviet Union inherited control of Central Asia and spent seventy years trying to transform the region into a compliant partner in the march toward expanding the Soviet empire.

When the Soviet Union dissolved in 1991, the five Soviet republics of Central Asia (which in many ways were less independent than the states of the United States, and certainly less developed economically) were suddenly independent nations. Since then, among the five new countries virtually every form of political and economic policy has been tried, from repressive dictatorship to democracy, from controlled economies to market capitalism. Whether the region is on the road to reform or to chaos remains to be seen.

Visitors to the Central Asian States see vestiges of all these periods and influences, from the yurts of the nomads to the glittering palaces of the new rulers. As the Central Asian States struggle to find their place among the nations of the world, it seems likely that the high drama that has so often characterized the region's history will continue to mark its future.

1

THE LAND AND PEOPLE

Central Asia is the heart of Eurasia—the world's largest land-mass—and consists of the independent nations of Kazakh-stan, Kyrgyzstan, Tajikistan, Turkmenistan, and Uzbekistan. Together, these five nations cover 1.5 million square miles— about 40 percent of the size of the United States. The region has no access to the ocean, though Kazakhstan and Turk-menistan are bordered on the west by the Caspian Sea. The region is surrounded on the north by Russia, on the east by China, and on the south by Iran and Afghanistan. Although most of Central Asia is flat desert or steppe (arid, treeless grassland), the region also contains some of the highest mountains in the world. Central Asia also includes some of the world's largest lakes. The region's diverse mountain, valley, and desert environments have created distinct lifestyles as inhab-itants have adapted to their surroundings.

THE FIVE NATIONS

The Central Asian States all lie in a single geographic region, the Aral Sea Basin, which is formed by the mountain and river system that drains into the Aral Sea, located in Kazakh-stan and Uzbekistan. Each country, however, has distinctive characteristics.

Kazakhstan, the northernmost of the Central Asian States, is also the largest. With just over 1 million square miles, it is almost four times the size of Texas and more than twice the size of the four other nations combined. The country shares a border with Russia to the north and shows the most Rus-sian influence of the five nations. It also borders the Caspian Sea, and about half of the Aral Sea is in Kazakh territory. Most of Kazakhstan is desert, semidesert, or steppe. Only 12 per-cent of the country is mountainous, chiefly in the Altay Shan and Tian Shan mountain ranges in the east and northeast. The Ural Mountains also extend southward from Russia into the northern part of Kazakhstan.

Turkmenistan is the second largest of the nations, with 188,456 square miles, slightly larger than California. Turkmenistan borders the Caspian Sea. Nearly 80 percent of the country lies within the Turan Depression, which includes the Kara-Kum Desert. The Pamir and Alai mountain ranges extend into the easternmost part of Turkmenistan. The country also shares the Kopet-Dag mountain range with Iran to the south.

Uzbekistan, the most populous of the Central Asian States, is the third largest, with 172,741 square miles. Uzbekistan is centrally located and is the only Central Asian nation to border all of the other four. Eighty percent of the country consists of flat plains or desert regions, including the Kyzyl-Kum Desert, which it shares with Kazakhstan. The most fertile region of the country is the Fergana Valley, which extends into Tajikistan and Kyrgyzstan. The southeastern portion of Uzbekistan contains the foothills of the Tian Shan mountain range. The country also includes the southern half of the Aral Sea.

Kyrgyzstan is the fourth largest of the nations, with 76,641 square miles—about the size of Nebraska. Kyrgyzstan is dominated by the Tian Shan, Pamir, and Alai mountain ranges. Tajikistan lies to the south of Kyrgyzstan. It is the smallest of the Central Asian States, with 55,251 square miles—about the size of Wisconsin. Tajikistan is also dominated by the Pamir and Alai mountain ranges, which cover 93 percent of its territory.

MOUNTAINS AND GLACIERS

Central Asia contains some of the highest mountain peaks in the world, many of them with elevations above twenty thousand feet. Called the "roof of the world," these lofty mountains include the Pamir, Alai, and Tian Shan ranges in southeastern Central Asia, and the Altay Shan range in northeastern Kazakhstan. In his book *The Central Asian States: Discovering Independence*, author Gregory Gleason describes the topography of Central Asia as

> an assemblage of towering mountains and deep valleys, of remote and impassable ridges, of high plateaus and glaciers. The Pamir, the Altai, the Tien Shan, and the Turkestan Ranges form a series of great radiating spirals in Central Asia. . . . No other inhabited landmass has so much sheer physicality, so many great mountains, so much earth thrusting into the skies. No other comparable area exists on earth.[1]

Hikers ascend the towering Tian Shan Mountains in southeastern Central Asia.

These mountains have defined the way people lived in the region throughout history. The plateaus and high valleys

support sheep and goat herding, while the valleys and oases at the base of the mountains support agriculture. Further away, the plains and deserts are fed by the melting snow and glaciers from the mountains.

The Pamir and Alai mountain ranges dominate Tajikistan's terrain. The highest point in Central Asia is Tajikistan's Communism Peak, in the Pamirs, with an elevation of 24,590 feet. The Pamir and Alai ranges contain many broad, grassy, treeless valleys (*pamir* means "pasture") and numerous glaciers. Glacier-fed streams and rivers have irrigated farmlands since ancient times.

The Tian Shan mountain range in Kyrgyzstan forms a natural border between Central Asia and China. These mountains consist of jagged crests and canyons that contain dense evergreen forests at lower elevations. The highest peaks in the Tian Shan (the highest of which is Pobeda Peak at 24,406 feet) range are covered with snow year-round. Runoff from snowmelt is the source of most of the rivers and streams in neighboring Kazakhstan. Most of Kyrgyzstan is dominated by the Pamir and Tian Shan ranges, which cover 65 percent of the country's land.

The Altay Shan mountains in northeastern Kazakhstan are made up of rolling meadows, rocky peaks, and pristine lakes and rivers. Many peaks in the Altay Shan are also snow-covered year-round. These mountains are the source of the Irtysh and Ob' Rivers in Kazakhstan.

The mountains of Central Asia contain many glaciers. There are sixty-five hundred glaciers in Kyrgyzstan alone, containing an estimated 928 billion cubic yards of water. The world's largest glacier outside of the polar regions is Tajikistan's Fedchenko Glacier, which covers more than 270 square miles. The runoff from glacier melt provides a source of water for many of Central Asia's rivers.

EARTHQUAKES

The mountains of Central Asia were formed over 100 million years ago, when the Indian subcontinent smashed into the Asian crustal plate. The mountains are still rising at a rate of nearly half an inch per year in the Tian Shan range. All this seismic activity makes Central Asia a major earthquake zone. A devastating earthquake destroyed the city of Ashkhabad, Turkmenistan, in 1948, and another earthquake hit the city of

THE GREAT EARTHQUAKES OF 1948 AND 1966

The earthquake that hit Ashkhabad, the capital of Turk-menistan, on October 6, 1948, registered nine on the Richter scale. The earthquake destroyed much of the city, including architectural monuments and mosques, and killed 110,000 people—a third of the city's population. It took five years to recover the bodies, clear the wreckage, and begin reconstruction, during which time the city was closed to outsiders. The city's many mosques were never rebuilt, and the Soviet reconstruction destroyed virtually all the old buildings that were left standing after the earthquake.

Another major earthquake leveled Uzbekistan's capital city, Tashkent, on April 25, 1966. Three hundred thousand people were left homeless. After the disaster, volunteers from the Soviet Union arrived to help rebuild the city, creating the fountains, plazas, and shady streets of present-day Tashkent.

However, the Soviet Union's announcement that 20 percent of the new apartments would be reserved for the Russian volunteers caused resentment among residents of Tashkent.

The 1966 Tashkent earthquake destroyed much of the city and left hundreds of thousands of people homeless.

Tashkent, Uzbekistan, in 1966. Numerous earthquakes measuring over six on the Richter scale rocked the city of Artush in the Kashgar region of Kyrgyzstan between 1996 and 1998. And earthquakes flattened homes and other buildings in the region along the Tajikistan-Afghanistan border in 1997 and 1998.

Unfortunately, earthquakes are sometimes followed by avalanches and mudslides. Overgrazing on the mountain slopes has increased the occurrence of mudslides and avalanches, which sometimes swallow entire villages. The 1989 earthquake that struck near Dushanbe, the capital of Tajikistan, caused a mudslide that killed hundreds of people in a nearby village.

DESERTS

In addition to having some of the loftiest mountains in the world, Central Asia also has some of the largest deserts. The huge Kara-Kum Desert, whose name means "black sands," lies to the south of the Aral Sea. The desert covers 135,000 square miles and includes most of Turkmenistan. In addition to dark-colored sand dunes whose crescent shapes are caused by the winds that sweep across it, the Kara-Kum has some vegetation, mostly saxaul bushes, and vast areas of flat cracked clay called *takyr*.

The Kyzyl-Kum Desert, whose name means "red sands," lies southeast of the Aral Sea. Its 115,000 square miles cover parts of Uzbekistan and Kazakhstan. Though they have distinct features, the Kara-Kum and Kyzyl-Kum can be considered a single desert ecosystem—combined they make up the fourth largest desert in the world. They have been inhabited for thousands of years by nomads skilled in the art of surviving in a demanding and often dangerous environment.

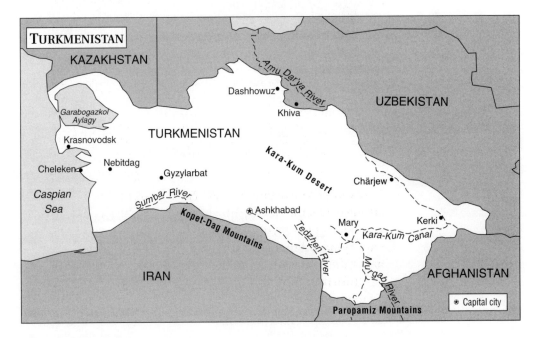

In a process known as desertification, the Kara-Kum and Kyzyl-Kum are expanding at a rapid rate. Approximately thirty-five hundred square miles of grassland in Central Asia turn to desert annually, a rate exceeded only by desertifica-

---

A CENTRAL ASIAN "HURRICANE"

On a visit to Ashkhabad, Turkmenistan, in 1989, American author Jonathon Maslow experienced just how changeable and violent the weather in Central Asia can be, as he explains in his book *Sacred Horses: Memoirs of a Turkmen Cowboy.* One night after a concert at the site of the town's ancient Silk Road caravansary (the inn where caravans stopped for the night), Maslow went into a courtyard. While he and a number of local people stood around smoking,

suddenly the bottom seemed to drop out of the gravity holding the Earth together, and from the desert a demonic wind attacked without mercy. One could feel the gaping jaws, the hot breath, the sharpened teeth. Some kind of white tree tassels swept across the courtyard like a blinding snowstorm. The water from the fountain, only a few seconds ago splashing tamely, stood up like wraiths in twisting, misshapen sheets. In another few seconds, a sandstorm was pelting the old caravansary, the tiny grains stinging our faces and hands. People lowered their heads, covered their faces with handkerchiefs, and fought to remain standing. In an instant the tranquil courtyard was blotted out in a terrifying whiteout. The wind whipped, whistled, and howled. A billion grains of sand rattled against the old protector of the caravans. You couldn't see where you were, you couldn't see where to go, and even if you could have, you couldn't get there. It was like a dry hurricane; if the wind and sand kept up like that for even half an hour, anyone caught out in the storm would perish. But in what must have been less than a minute, it was gone, like an ominous warning from the desert to caravan travelers dead hundred of years.

When I found Dr. Shikhmurad [Maslow's host], parked waiting for me on the street side of the municipal theater, I found out that Turkmen call such a wind "Urugan"—an amazing cognate of the Amerindian name for the evil spirit of such storms, Hurakan, which Spanish expeditions from Columbus on learned in the Caribbean; it was later incorporated into English as "hurricane."

tion in Africa. Desertification is due to climatic conditions such as wind erosion and to land mismanagement such as pollution, overgrazing of livestock, and massive irrigation runoff. When water leaks from irrigation canals, salt is brought to the surface and salt marshes form. These marshes dry into unusable clay flats, which are further eroded by the wind. Desertification reduces crop yields and causes a widespread loss of plant and animal life, loss of arable land, and destruction of historical and cultural monuments.

RIVERS

Through the vast deserts flow Central Asia's two main rivers, the Amu Dar'ya and Syr Dar'ya (*dar'ya* means "river" in Persian). Over the millennia, the Amu and Syr have formed two massive river basins that collect much of the rainfall in the region, which then flows toward the Aral Sea. The Amu and Syr and the smaller rivers that flow into them have been used for irrigation for centuries, but in the second half of the twentieth century so much water was diverted for agriculture that the Aral Sea began to dry up. The resulting soil erosion fills the rivers with mud and makes them difficult to navigate and makes irrigation canals difficult to maintain.

The Amu is the longest river in Central Asia, flowing 1,578 miles from the Pamir Mountains to the southern shore of the Aral Sea. It forms the boundary between Tajikistan and northeastern Afghanistan and also flows through Turkmenistan and Uzbekistan. It is navigable for about nine hundred miles. Pollution in the form of industrial and agricultural waste has seeped into the river, and there are elevated levels of phenol and oil by-products that endanger the health of the people who rely on it for drinking water.

The Syr River is the second longest. Its principal tributary is the Naryn River, which arises in the mountains of Kyrgyzstan. The Syr flows 1,370 miles through Tajikistan, Uzbekistan, and Kazakhstan. Though heavily polluted by agricultural, industrial, and municipal wastes, it is also used as a drinking-water source by many communities and is a major source of irrigation water in the Fergana Valley.

THE FERGANA VALLEY

The Fergana Valley lies to the east of the Kyzyl-Kum Desert and covers 8,270 square miles in parts of Uzbekistan, Tajikistan, and Kyrgyzstan. The valley is bounded by mountain ranges to the north, south, and east and by the Syr River to the west. It is the most densely populated region in Central Asia. With rivers bringing rich soil deposits from the mountains, it is also the most fertile part of Central Asia and supports large-scale agriculture. Throughout history, the people living in the Fergana Valley have been sedentary farmers. Since the late nineteenth century, much of the land has been used for growing cotton. Because the Fergana Valley overlaps the territory of three nations, there is friction over control of its land and water resources.

LAKES AND SEAS

Central Asia's lakes and seas face many ecological problems such as pollution from industrial waste and shrinkage due to overirrigation. Another threat to the environment comes from flooding, particularly in the Caspian Sea.

The Caspian Sea, which lies between Europe and Asia, borders Kazakhstan and Turkmenistan. Covering 143,550 square miles, it is the largest inland body of water in the world. Beneath this salt lake lie oil and natural gas deposits that are eagerly sought by all the nations that lay claim to it. Complicating the development of the oil and gas industry is the fact that the water level has been rising since 1978, and 2.5 million acres of land in Kazakhstan have been flooded. Pollution caused by drilling operations has added to the millions of tons of wastes that have flowed into the sea. Thus, the Caspian Sea is rapidly becoming an ecological disaster area.

The Aral Sea, which lies on the border between western Uzbekistan and southern Kazakhstan, is the largest body of water within Central Asia. It was the world's fourth largest inland sea before 1960; since then, diversion of water for irrigation has shrunk the Aral by nearly half. It is also heavily polluted from chemicals used in agriculture. Its shores are steppe or desert and uninhabited except for Uzbekistan, to the south.

Lake Issyk-Kul in Kyrgyzstan is the second largest body of water in Central Asia. It covers 2,355 square miles in northeastern Kyrgyzstan at the base of the Tian Shan Mountains and is fed by the Chu, a seasonal river that evaporates in the summer. Lake Issyk-Kul, whose name means "warm lake" in the Kyrgyz language, does not freeze in the winter. Like the Aral Sea, the lake has been shrinking steadily because of the diversion of inflowing streams for irrigation.

Lake Balkhash is a 376-mile-long lake in southeastern Kazakhstan. Partially saline and partially fresh, the lake is fed by the Ili River and is frozen from November to March. Pollution from copper smelters that were set up on the shores of Lake Balkhash in the 1930s has affected wildlife in the area, although the lake still supports a fishing industry.

CLIMATE

The climate of Central Asia tends to be continental, with cold, frosty winters and hot, dry summers, but the climates of the mountain, valley, desert, plateau, and glacier areas vary widely. In the Kara-Kum Desert in summer, daytime temperatures often reach 120 degrees Fahrenheit but may fall by as much as 80 degrees at night. There is heavy snowfall in the north and east and continuous winter snow cover in many of the mountainous areas of Kyrgyzstan and Tajikistan, where temperatures fall as low as –50 degrees. Summers in the mountains, however, are mild, making them a favorite vacation spot for city dwellers in the desert regions.

High winds are a constant threat in the desert and steppe regions of Central Asia. Huge sandstorms can arrive without warning. They make travel impossible, flatten buildings, and even cover them with sand.

CAPITALS AND MAJOR CITIES

Climate has been a major factor in the selection of sites for the cities of Central Asia. The first requirement for a city is water. In the deserts of Turkmenistan and Kazakhstan, where rain is infrequent, cities are often far apart and located along rivers or near reliable wells. In the mountainous regions of Kyrgyzstan, Tajikistan, and Uzbekistan, where rain and snowfall are more plentiful and there are many small rivers, lakes, and springs, towns and villages are closer together. But everywhere in Central Asia, the growth and importance of cities often depended on their role in Silk Road commerce. Some of the more important cities founded along the Silk Road include Samarqand, Bukhara, and Tashkent in Uzbekistan and Merv in Turkmenistan.

Samarqand is one of the oldest cities in Central Asia. It was Alexander the Great's base for two years during his conquest of Central Asia in the fourth century B.C., and Tamerlane

ARAL: THE SHRINKING SEA

Once the fourth largest inland sea in the world, the Aral has been shrinking steadily since the 1960s. At that time, there was a sharp increase in the amount of water diverted from the sea's main tributaries, the Amu and Syr Rivers, for the irrigation of cotton fields. Between 1960 and 1980, the amount of water diverted from the rivers doubled. In addition, the Kara-Kum Canal—the world's longest—carries away one-fourth of the water that would otherwise flow into the Aral. This and other irrigation projects have virtually eliminated inflow to the Aral, resulting in a depletion of the water level and rapid shrinkage of its area to about half its former size.

Between 1966 and 1993 the Aral Sea's eastern and southern borders had receded by up to fifty miles, and its volume shrank by 75 percent. The sea split in two in 1987, forming a larger southern sea and a smaller northern one. Each of these seas is only sometimes reached by one of the rivers. The northern end has since formed a separate lake, which has been dubbed the Little Aral Sea. A Central Asian woman related her memory of the Little Aral Sea for author Simon Richmond in the book *Central Asia:* "As a child I remember learning to swim here. My father said, you live by the sea, so you must learn. When I told my children this, they didn't believe me. 'Where is the sea?' they asked."

made it into the capital of the Mongol Empire in the four-teenth century.

Bukhara, east of the Amu River in central Uzbekistan, was the capital of the Shaybanid khanate in the sixteenth century and had a brief period of independence in the early 1920s. It was known as the Bukhara People's Republic but became part of the Uzbek Soviet Socialist Republic in 1924. Today it is the site of many historic buildings that the government is working hard to preserve.

Merv, once one of the most important Muslim cities, was destroyed by Mongols in the early thirteenth century; all its citizens, perhaps as many as a million people, were slaugh-tered. It was destroyed again in 1795 by the emir of Bukhara. Altogether, over the last twenty-six hundred years, five walled cities stood there. Present-day Merv is both a vast archaeo-logical site and a modern city.

Since prehistoric times, civilization in Central Asia has de-pended on rivers with a permanent water flow, especially the Amu and Syr, but today the towns along their banks are mostly agricultural and small to medium in size. Tashkent was founded on a tributary of the Syr River in the first cen-tury B.C. The capital of Uzbekistan, Tashkent is the largest and most diverse city in Central Asia. Its 2000 population count of approximately 2.3 million includes large groups of Russians, Koreans, Caucasians, and Tatars.

Almaty, located just south of the Ili River, was the capital of Kazakhstan until December 1998, when government offices were moved to Astana, a more central location. Almaty remains the focus of commerce and culture in Kazakhstan, however, and is the most Russian of all Central Asian cities, having been founded by the Russians in 1854.

Bishkek, on the Chu River, is the capital of Kyrgyzstan. With a population of 800,000, it is also the commercial center of the country and the hub of the relatively prosperous Chu Valley. Bishkek has a large population of ethnic Russians as a result of Soviet decisions to move industries to the area during World War II and the cold war.

Dushanbe, the capital of Tajikistan, was the site of many violent demonstrations and riots during the 1990s. Dushanbe was little more than a market town until it became part of a rail line route in 1929 and the Soviet Union decided to make it a center for cotton and silk processing—and the capital of the new Tajik Soviet Socialist Republic. Its 700,000 people have had to endure more civil unrest since independence than those in any of the other Central Asian States. The problems stem from the natural and cultural divisions that characterize Tajikistan: Dushanbe, in the west-central part of the country, is cut off from the Gorno-Badakhshan region in the east by the Pamir Mountains and cut off from the

Bukhara, in central Uzbekistan, is the site of many historic buildings, such as the Kalon Minaret, which was built during the Middle Ages.

Fergana Valley in the north by the Fan Mountains. In addition, the Tajik majority is split into several clan and political factions that have frequently battled one another and the large Uzbek minority.

Ashkhabad, the capital of Turkmenistan, has been reconstructed twice after being destroyed by massive earthquakes in the first century B.C. and in 1948. Today it is a relatively small and quiet capital with a population of just over half a million. It is increasingly dominated by the building program of the country's president, Saparmurat Niyazov, who calls

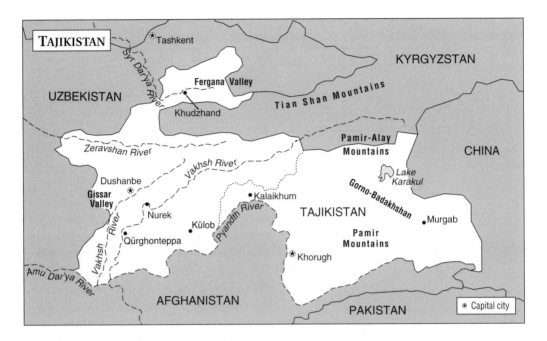

himself Turkmenbashi, leader of the Turkmen. He has built a huge presidential palace, an Arch of Neutrality with a forty-foot-high rotating statue of himself on the top, a new National Museum, and what will be the world's largest fountain.

THE PEOPLE OF CENTRAL ASIA

The five dominant ethnic groups in Central Asia are the Kazakh, Kyrgyz, Tajik, Turkmen, and Uzbek. In general, each group is in the majority in the nation named after it. However, the Kazakhs are barely a majority in Kazakhstan because of extensive colonization by Russia, and each state has minorities of the other ethnic groups, sometimes in significant numbers.

The ancestors of the Kyrgyz people were nomadic herders in the northern part of Central Asia whose Persian culture mixed with that of the Turks—pastoral nomads who came into Central Asia from the north and the south beginning in the ninth century. There is a very close cultural and linguistic connection between the Kyrgyz and Kazakh peoples. The Kazakhs emerged in the fifteenth century when clan leaders split away from the Uzbeks in search of their own land. They settled in present-day southeastern Kazakhstan. The Kyrgyz and Kazakh languages have Turkic roots and show both Tatar and Mongol influences.

Tajiks are descendants of ancient Persian inhabitants of Central Asia and a mixture of various Turkic and Mongol peoples. The Tajik language and culture is based on Iranian roots rather than Turkic. Uzbek clan leaders were Islamized descendants of the Mongols who left southern Siberia and settled in what is now Uzbekistan in the fifteenth century. The Tajik and Uzbek peoples lived in close proximity to one another and often used each other's language throughout history. They did not think of themselves as separate nationalities, and it was not until the USSR imposed rather arbitrary labels on them in the 1920s that they were forced to make a distinction.

Turkmen are believed to be descendants of displaced nomadic horse-breeding clans who arrived in the Kara-Kum Desert at the beginning of the Seljuq Empire in the late tenth century. Today Turkmen make up around 80 percent of Turkmenistan's population, and clan loyalty remains extremely important to them.

A sixth ethnic group, the Karakalpaks, were a nomadic and fishing people who were first recorded in history in the sixteenth century. They share cultural and linguistic ties with Kazakhs, Uzbeks, and Kyrgyz. The Karakalpak people were given their own land in 1936, when the Soviet Union created the Karakalpak Autonomous Republic (also known as Karakalpakstan) within Uzbekistan. Now, however, Karakalpaks are a minority in the region named for them because of an influx of ethnic Uzbeks and Kazakhs. In addition, Karakalpakstan, once a thriving agricultural area, has become one of the poorest parts of Uzbekistan because the shrinking of the Aral Sea has led to extensive soil erosion and salinization.

Ethnic identity has always been important to the people of Central Asia. Throughout history, ethnic alliance has played a larger role in the lives and politics of Central Asians than nationality has. Today people of the region are often unsure whether to identify themselves by their ethnicity or their nationality.

In addition to these primary ethnic groups, Central Asia also has significant minority populations of people from foreign countries who emigrated or were relocated to the region. A wave of Russian, Ukrainian, Tatar, and Cossack settlers arrived in the nineteenth century during Russian colonization. Greeks form a considerable minority in Uzbek-

istan, where they were relocated by the Soviets from the Crimea before and during World War II. Other Greeks immigrated to the region after the end of the Greek Civil War in 1949. During and just after World War II, Koreans, Kurds, Volga Germans, and Crimean Tatars were deported to Central Asia by the Soviets, and many Jews came to the region as refugees from Nazi Germany.

These children belong to the Turkmen ethnic group, one of five dominant ethnic groups in Central Asia.

For more than two thousand years, Central Asia's location between East Asia and Europe has made it both a battleground and a fertile field for cultural exchange and innovation. In the twenty-first century, the region's new nations are again in a pivotal role. They have the opportunity to show how diverse ethnic and religious groups can live and work together, how peoples accustomed to farming and herding can learn new ways of making a living, and how societies with few democratic traditions can accommodate the new freedoms that many in Central Asia hope to achieve.

2

FROM THE SILK ROAD TO THE FALL OF THE SOVIET UNION

Central Asia's geographic location as the midpoint between Europe and Asia has predisposed it throughout history to trade, invasions, and an influx of foreign cultures, languages, and religions. The first major contact between Central Asia and the West was the conquest of the region by Alexander the Great in the fourth century B.C. But even before then, there was a thriving network of trade routes that ran through Central Asia, providing the principal means of commerce between China and Europe for many centuries. The history of invasions, civil and tribal wars, religious conflicts, colonization, and, above all, commerce, shaped the development of the region through the twentieth century.

THE HISTORY OF THE SILK ROAD

Trade and commerce between the Mediterranean region and China existed as far back as 2000 B.C. but began to flourish at the end of the second century B.C., when Chinese merchants began traveling regularly into Central Asia. Chang Ch'ien, a Chinese diplomat who returned from Central Asia in 138 B.C., reported to the Han emperor of China that "the region has many fine horses . . .; their forebears are supposed to have been foaled from heavenly horses."[2] The Han emperor was eager to obtain these so-called heavenly horses, which probably came from the Fergana Valley in modern-day Uzbekistan, and merchants in Central Asia and Europe were interested in silk from China. Caravans began to travel along overland routes, trading at various outposts along the way. However, despite centuries of trade in the region, the term "Silk Road" was not used until the nineteenth century, when a German geographer named Ferdinand von Richthofen coined the term when Europeans and Russians displayed a renewed interest in this ancient trade route.

The Silk Road was not just one road. Rather, it was a complex network of routes that met and diverged at various places along the way and expanded through the centuries. The easternmost point of the route was Kaifeng in China. From there the route headed west, forking at China's Taklimakan Desert, with one route skirting to the north and one to the south. The routes met again at Kashgar in China, then threaded through a series of high mountain passes in the Pamir and Tian Shan ranges in Central Asia. Branches of the route continued westward through the Fergana Valley, through the cities of Kokand, Samarqand, Tashkent, Bukhara, and Merv in modern-day Uzbekistan and Turkmenistan. Other branches also went into India, Iran, and Russia. The overland routes ended at the Black Sea and the Mediterranean Sea, where goods were then shipped to Europe.

Trade goods were carted by camels, horses, mules, donkeys, and yaks, with caravans covering up to thirty miles a day. Ruy Gonzáles de Clavijo, a fifteenth-century Spanish ambassador to Samarqand, gave the following account of items that were traded along the Silk Road:

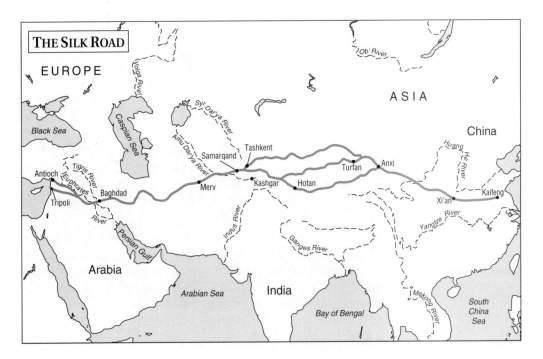

Russia and Tartary send linen and skins; China sends silks, which are the best in the world, (more especially the satins), and musk, which is found in no other part of the world, rubies and diamonds, pearls and rhubarb, and many other things. The merchandise which comes from China is the best and most precious which comes to this city [Samarqand], and they say that the people of China are the most skilful workmen in the world. . . . From India come spices, such as nutmegs, cloves, mace, cinnamon, ginger, and many others.[3]

Most merchants and caravans did not travel the entire length of the Silk Road in a single trip. Instead, traders from Europe, Iran, India, and China met at various stopping points along the way—particularly in Central Asia, which lay halfway between Europe and China. Goods changed hands

Merchants and caravans traveling the Silk Road often stopped in Central Asia, the halfway point between Europe and China.

many times along the Silk Road, and by the time they reached their final destination the buyers had no idea who the original sellers were. Cities such as Bukhara and Samarqand thrived as bartering centers on the Silk Road, offering travelers food and lodging, stables, marketplaces, brokers to set up contracts, and banks to extend credit. Central Asia thus became a powerful commercial and cultural center.

The trading that took place along the Silk Road included more than just material goods. Tribes migrated along the routes, and diplomats, scholars, and missionaries traveled alongside merchants in the overland caravans. Central Asia became the center for a vast exchange of ideas, cultures, languages, religions, literature, and technology. The region became a religious and cultural melting pot, and although today it is predominantly Muslim it was once one of the most religiously diverse regions on earth. Before the rise of Islam in the region, Christianity, Judaism, Buddhism, Zoroastrianism, and Manichaeism all coexisted.

This overland trading thrived until the turbulence of the Mongol invasions in the thirteenth and fourteenth centuries led to a gradual dropoff in the use of the route. After the establishment of ocean trade routes from Europe to India and China beginning in the early sixteenth century, trading along the old Silk Road steadily declined.

THE EARLY KINGDOMS
Though trade routes through Central Asia were probably in use as long as four thousand years ago, the recorded history of the region began in the sixth century B.C. At that time, the Achaemenid Empire of Iran included three kingdoms beyond the Amu River: Sogdiana, Khorezm, and Saka. Sogdiana was the land between the Amu and Syr Rivers and consisted of separate oasis states, including the cities of Samarqand and Bukhara in modern-day Uzbekistan. The Sogdians were sedentary farmers who spoke an Iranian language that is still spoken in remote areas of Tajikistan. Khorezm occupied an area along the lower reaches of the Amu and south of the Aral Sea. Saka extended over the Central Asian steppes beyond the Syr and included the Tian Shan mountain range. The nomadic Saka clans were some of the earliest inhabitants of what are now Kyrgyzstan and Kazakhstan. These three kingdoms were subjected to repeated invasions and came under

Alexander the Great's influence on Central Asia was considerable, and today he is regarded as a folk hero in the region.

the control of several powers throughout their history. The first European conquest of the region was by the kingdom of Macedon.

ALEXANDER THE GREAT

By the mid-fourth century B.C. Central Asia contained many city-states and was still under the control of the Achaemenid Empire. In 329 B.C. Alexander of Macedon, known as Alexander the Great, advanced through the region on his way to conquer India. He crossed the Amu River, taking Samarqand, and then crossed the Syr River. There, he was met by warrior clans of the Saka people. The Sakas allied with the Sogdians and managed to hold the mountain regions during eighteen months of guerrilla warfare before surrendering to Alexander's army. To cement relations with the Macedonians, a local chieftain offered his daughter into captivity and marriage with Alexander.

Alexander conquered Central Asian cities as far east as Hojent in what is now northern Tajikistan. The city, like many others in the region, was renamed in his honor. Although Alexander died in 323 B.C., his brief influence in Central Asia was significant. Greek culture and customs remained for centuries, and today Alexander is seen as a folk hero in the region. Uzbekistan lays claim to his tomb, as do Egypt and Pakistan.

CENTURIES OF CONQUEST

Following the conquest by the Macedonian Empire, many invaders—Chinese, Sakas, Kushans, Indians, Sassanids, Huns, Sogdians, Turks, Arabs, and Mongols—battled the indigenous peoples and each other for control of the region. Greek rule in Bactria, which was a large empire covering what are now Uzbekistan and northern Afghanistan, lasted two centuries before it succumbed to nomadic incursions of the Sakas and other steppe peoples. Saka rule lasted about a century before the Kushan Empire arose in the first century

B.C. The Kushans were also greatly influenced by Greek culture. They controlled the trade routes of the Silk Road until late in the first century B.C., when Iranian Parthians took control of northwestern India and western Central Asia. In the second century A.D., the Sassanids took control of Sogdiana from the Kushans.

In the fourth century A.D. the Sassanids lost their Asian possessions to the Huns. In 559, the Sassanids allied with the Turks, from southern Siberia, and ousted the Huns. Over the next few centuries, the Turks controlled the region, and their culture mixed with the Sogdian culture. The rule of the Turks faded late in the seventh century, and in the eighth century Arabic incursions brought a new rule to the land, that of Islam.

THE RISE OF ISLAM

Islam was founded by the prophet Muhammad in the city of Mecca, in what is now Saudi Arabia. In 610, Muhammad began dictating the scriptures that became the Qur'an, the Islamic holy book. Following Muhammad's death in 632, Muslims (adherents of Islam) began traveling to spread their religion. In 642, Muslim armies reached the region known as Transoxiana—the land between the Amu and Syr Rivers in what is now Turkmenistan. There, they defeated the Turks and took the city of Merv. In addition to spreading their faith, Muslim armies sought Arab dominance of trade throughout the region. In the early eighth century, Bukhara, Samarqand, and Kashgar fell to Muslim rule.

Arab control of the Silk Road trade routes was challenged by the Chinese Tang dynasty in the mid–eighth century. Following the murder of the leader of the Tashkent Turks by the Chinese, the Turks, Arabs, and Tibetans joined to battle against the Chinese in 751 at the Battle of the Talas River. The Chinese were defeated and left Central Asia. Since then, Islam and Islamic culture have dominated the region.

Muslim armies now ruled the western half of the Silk Road, controlling not only trade but politics and religion as well. It was the Muslim dominance of trade that helped spread their religion in urban areas along the Silk Road, and then gradually to the rural areas. Central Asians converted to Islam for a number of reasons in addition to the spiritual—often it was politically, economically, or socially advantageous to convert to the religion of the majority in the region. Regardless of the motivation, over the next few centuries many thousands of Central Asians converted to Islam.

Beginning in the ninth century, Arab rule in Central Asia was challenged by local rebellions and wars between various dynasties, each seeking to control the region. These dynasties included the Sāmānid, Ghaznavid, Karakhanid, Seljuq, Karakitay, and Khorezmshah. Parts of Central Asia shifted back and forth between these warring factions, each of which ruled briefly during the next few centuries. The Khorezmshahs gained control of Transoxiana in the mid–twelfth century and were still in power when the Mongols arrived in Central Asia from China in the early thirteenth century.

THE MONGOL EMPIRE

The Mongols, under the leadership of Genghis Khan, had already conquered northern China by 1218. In that year, representatives of Genghis Khan arrived in the city of Otyrar in modern-day Kazakhstan to open trade between the Mongol and Muslim empires. The governor of Otyrar, however, fearing that the Mongols were spies planning an invasion, had them arrested and executed. In retaliation for the murders, Genghis Khan advanced into Central Asia with an estimated 200,000 soldiers and sacked the cities of Otyrar, Khudzhand,

---

SAMARQAND IN THE SEVENTH CENTURY

In 646 a Chinese monk named Xuanzang wrote the *Buddhist Records of the Western World*, which contains references to seventh-century Central Asia. Susan Whitfield quotes Xuanzang's description of the independent city-state of Samarqand in the book *Life Along the Silk Road*.

> The country of Samarkand is about 500 miles in circumference and broader from east to west than from north to south. The capital is six miles or so in circumference, completely enclosed by rugged land and very populous. The precious merchandise of many foreign countries is stored here. The soil is rich and productive and yields abundant harvests. The forest trees afford a thick vegetation and flowers and fruit are plentiful. *Shen* horses are bred here. The inhabitants' skill in the arts and trades exceeds that of other countries. The climate is agreeable and temperate and the people brave and energetic.

and Bukhara. The Mongols then conquered Samarqand, Merv, and Termiz.

Genghis Khan's descendants eventually conquered most of Eurasia. Their empire included China, Russia, Central Asia, and the Middle East. The Mongol devastation of conquered cities struck a blow to Central Asian civilization that would last for centuries. An early-fourteenth-century traveler to Samarqand described the ruination of the once-great city: "There were formerly great palaces on its bank, and constructions which bear witness to the lofty aspirations of the townsfolk, but most of this is obliterated, and most of the city has also fallen into ruins. It has no city wall [after the Mongol devastation the walls presumably had not been rebuilt] and gates."[4] Samarqand was later rebuilt by Timur the Lame, also known as Tamerlane, a descendant of Genghis Khan, who made the city his capital and a center of culture in the late fourteenth century. Timur's tomb still stands in Samarqand.

Thirteenth-century Mongol leader Genghis Khan.

Timur died in 1405, and his descendants continued to rule for another century. Mongol rule faded as various empires and clans again vied for control of Central Asia. The sedentary Uzbeks and nomadic Kazakhs fought each other during the fourteenth to sixteenth centuries, with the Kazakhs gaining control of the steppe region. The Zhungarians briefly took control of Central Asia from 1635 to 1758. After the death of the last Zhungarian emperor, the Kazakhs, who had been weakened during the reign of the Zhungarians, gradually began to accept Russian protection against other warring clans. To the Russians, this meant that they had the right to annex the region they were protecting, thus setting the stage for the Russian colonization of Central Asia that would begin at the turn of the nineteenth century.

RUSSIAN COLONIALISM

After the Kazakh region was annexed in the mid–eighteenth century, Russian Tatars and Cossacks began to arrive to settle and farm the land. The Kazakhs revolted against these immigrants who were taking over their lands, and as a result of their revolt the Russians stripped the Kazakhs of their autonomy and officially made their land into a Russian colony.

THE HEAD OF TIMUR THE LAME

Timur died in 1405 and was buried in the Gur Emir Mausoleum, which still stands in Samarqand. Three of his sons, a grandson, and a sheikh were also buried in the crypt beneath the mausoleum. According to an account in Edgar Knobloch's book *Beyond the Oxus*, when the Soviet Archaeological Commission opened the crypt in 1941, they

> found here the skeleton of a man who, though lame in both right limbs, must have been of powerful physique, tall for a Tartar and of a haughty bearing. They examined the skeleton and the remains, which included fragments of muscle and skin, and some hair of the head, eye-brows, red moustache and beard. The skull indicated Mongol features.

The Soviet anthropologist Mikhail Gerazimov used this skull to reconstruct the head of Timur, so today historians have a good idea what the famous Mongol leader looked like.

The Russians began to colonize other parts of Central Asia early in the nineteenth century. Because of fears of British expansion from India, the Russians wanted a secure southern border. In addition, they had expansionist ideas of their own and wanted to build a Russian Empire to rival the British Empire. The Russian army turned toward Central Asia, which lay between their southern border and India. One by one, Central Asian cities were assaulted and fell to Russian forces; by 1885, the entire region was under Russian control.

The Russians exploited the Central Asian colonies, using them as a source of raw material and cheap labor. In 1861, when the U.S. Civil War interrupted the exportation of cotton from the American South, Russia turned to Central Asia, where cotton had been cultivated as far back as the Middle Ages. Russian manufacturing industries also exploited the region's vast natural resources.

In the late nineteenth century, Russian immigrants began to flood into Central Asia, seeking land of their own. At this time, there was a Russian policy of noninterference, so the influx of chiefly middle-class immigrants remained segregated from the local populations. The immigrants did not learn the traditions or languages of their new land, and the native population was not encouraged to learn Russian. However, the Russians brought many cultural and technological advances with them, such as trains, telegraphs, telephones, gas lights, and hotels. As a result, Central Asian cities were transformed into modern cities during Russian colonialism.

With the outbreak of World War I in 1914, Central Asian cattle, cotton, and food were requisitioned for the Russian war effort. When the Russian czar (ruler) demanded that Central Asian men be conscripted into the Russian imperial army, there was a rebellion. Violent uprisings began in 1916, starting in the city of Tashkent and moving eastward. There were bloody reprisals against the Kazakhs and Kyrgyz, many of whom fled toward China.

The Russian Revolution of 1917 brought hope for social reform to many people in Central Asia. They wanted to coexist peacefully with Bolshevik Russia, but by early 1918 the Red Army marched into Qŭqon and sacked the town, slaughtering five thousand people and toppling their independent government. Other Central Asian cities were captured by the Red Army as well, and by the mid-1920s Central Asia was firmly under the rule of the Soviet Union.

THE SOVIET ERA

The Soviet Union feared that a unified Central Asia would create a sense of nationalism that would threaten its rule of the region. In other words, a united Central Asia might be large and powerful enough to challenge Soviet dominance. The Soviet solution was to divide the region. In the mid-1920s the current national boundaries were drawn and the five republics, none of which had existed independently prior to that time, were created. When ethnic and linguistic differences were considered at all, they were used to introduce enough instability so that Moscow would be needed to settle disputes. Groups found themselves fragmented by the new borders. Ethnic groups who shared much in common in terms of history, customs, and traditions were differentiated and renamed by the Soviets, so people suddenly had to decide whether they were "Tajik" or "Uzbek," for instance, when they had never before thought of themselves in those terms. The Soviets also forcibly relocated groups of people, creating pockets of ethnic groups. For example, a sizable Uzbek minority still exists in Kyrgyzstan and Turkmenistan.

Beginning in the late 1920s, collectivized agriculture was forcibly imposed on Central Asia. Under the leadership of Joseph Stalin, the Soviets put an end to private land ownership and organized agricultural communes. When there were not enough experienced farmers available to work on the communes, the Soviets forced some nomadic Kazakhs and Kyrgyz to become farmers. People slaughtered livestock to protest Stalin's agricultural policies, and this led to widespread famines in the 1920s and '30s. During this time, thousands of people perished from malnutrition and disease.

Resistance to the implementation of collectivized agriculture, as well as to other Communist policies, was met by brutal political repression in the 1920s and '30s, with a renewed wave of repression after World War II. These so-called Stalinist purges consisted of roundups, deportations, and mass executions of political dissenters. Many Central Asians who expressed nationalist ideas, including writers, intellectuals, and political figures, were targeted.

A Central Asian collective farm worker drives a tractor through the mud in this 1920s photograph.

The Soviet era was also one of religious repression in Central Asia. During the Russian colonial period, there were few attempts to interfere with the religious practices of the Muslims. This policy changed under the Soviets, who saw religion

as subversive to their own control. From the late 1920s to the late 1930s many Muslims were killed, and Islamic courts and schools were closed. The Soviet government also forbade the hajj, or pilgrimage to Mecca, and the publishing of the Qur'an. During the 1970s and '80s, Islamic mosques in Central Asia were converted for secular (nonreligious) use, and the religious significance of Islamic traditions was officially downplayed. Despite decades of government repression, Islam remained an important part of the lives and identities of Central Asian Muslims throughout the Soviet era.

The Soviets brought further changes to Central Asia during World War II (1939–1945). During this time, factories were relocated from battle areas in the western portions of the Soviet Union to the more remote areas of the Central Asian Soviet Socialist Republics, out of harm's way. These factories, which remained after the war, brought heavy industry into the region. Refugees also poured into the region during the war years. Many of them, including Volga Germans and Chechens, were deported by Stalin out of fear that they would help the Soviets' enemies, and they now form sizable minorities in Central Asia.

A Communist-era mural depicts Soviet leader Joseph Stalin (top right). The scratched-out image of a high-ranking Soviet official (center) is evidence of a Stalinist purge.

Throughout the Soviet era, the Communist officials' mismanagement of land and resources led to widespread environmental devastation in Central Asia. Overgrazing of livestock in the grasslands of the steppes region destroyed the natural habitat. Cotton and grain were widely grown to meet the needs of the other Soviet republics, and a failure to rotate crops depleted the soil. Further damage to the soil and environment resulted from the massive irrigation needed to support these crops. Water was diverted from the Amu and Syr Rivers for decades, leading to a gradual depletion of the Aral Sea. Pesticides, defoliants, and fertilizers that were used in agriculture polluted the water supply and reduced the nutritional value of food grown in the region, causing serious health problems. The Soviet Union also carried out nuclear testing in Central Asia, causing further ecological and environmental problems. The area around the Semey Nuclear Testing site in Kazakhstan has excessive levels of radiation, and abandoned uranium mines in Tajikistan and Kyrgyzstan leak radiation and contaminate the groundwater.

Central Asia saw an increase in heavy industry during World War II when many factories were relocated there from battle areas in the western regions of the Soviet Union.

Despite the political and religious repression and the ecological devastation of the Soviet era, Central Asia did see some improvements during this time. The overall standard of living rose, especially the quality and availability of health care. Millions of Central Asians were employed by Soviet industrial and agricultural concerns. There was also a boom in education, especially in the sciences, and literacy rose to close to 100 percent in all five republics. Languages were given a standardized form during the Soviet era, and the Kyrgyz language was given an alphabet for the first time.

THE BREAKUP OF THE SOVIET UNION

After Mikhail Gorbachev became leader of the Soviet Union in 1985, he introduced the new policies of glasnost, which permitted open discussion of political issues and more freedom of the press, and perestroika, a restructuring of the Soviet economy and government. Gorbachev's reforms led to social

Mikhail Gorbachev's push for reform in the Soviet Union eventually led to a movement toward independence in many of the Soviet republics.

upheaval, protest, and rapid movement toward independence in many of the Soviet republics. As Soviet rule began to crumble in the late 1980s, political opposition groups began to form in Central Asia. Anti-Communist demonstrations and riots became increasingly common. There was also a surge in violence among various ethnic groups in 1989 and 1990.

In August 1991 an attempted coup in the Soviet Union, in which Communist hard-liners tried to oust Gorbachev, failed. After the failed coup, Uzbekistan and Kyrgyzstan immediately declared their independence from the Soviet Union, followed by Tajikistan in September and Turkmenistan in October. In December 1991 Kazakhstan became the last of the Central Asian republics to declare its independence. The USSR had officially dissolved by this time. Though none had ever existed independently before, the Central Asian States now found themselves suddenly thrust into the role of sovereign nations.

3

THE INDEPENDENT STATES OF CENTRAL ASIA

The breakup of the Soviet Union had been anticipated in Central Asia since the mid-1980s. Even before the USSR fell apart, the five republics of Central Asia had declared that their laws would take precedence over Soviet laws, but decades of domination by Moscow left them with few resources and little experience in self-government. Ethnic conflicts flared as groups vied for local and national dominance. The period since independence has been marked by an often unsuccessful search for ways to redefine ethnic, national, and regional identities that will lead to peace, political stability, and economic prosperity. Although the region's common cultural and historical elements have helped to prevent serious conflicts among the new nations, there have been significant divergences and disagreements since independence.

Kazakhstan retains the closest ties with Russia, and its president, Nursultan Nazarbayev, is the best-known politician in the region. At one point President Nazarbayev proposed a virtual reunion with Russia. Though that plan has been abandoned, Kazakhstan still relies on Russia in many ways. In contrast, Kyrgyzstan was the first of the Soviet republics to declare independence. It adopted a new Western-style constitution in 1993 and instituted aggressive economic reforms. These steps made observers in the United States and Europe think that the Kyrgyz government would abandon the oppressive policies of the Soviet era. However, in 2000 its democratic reforms seemed to falter as the press and opposition political leaders were harassed by the government.

Uzbekistan is the most populous of the Central Asian States and tends to present itself as the leader of the new nations. It has long been a major producer of cotton, but toward the end of the Soviet era, a massive case of fraud and embezzlement was uncovered among bureaucrats who controlled cotton farming. Many of the old Communist bureaucrats, however, have retained power, and the leader of the fraud plot was pardoned. In many ways, little has changed in Uzbekistan since independence. This is also true of Turkmenistan, which was the most reluctant to leave the USSR—it essentially waited until there was no USSR left to be part of. Turkmenistan is now a one-party state headed by Saparmurat Niyazov, who has banned opposition parties and newspapers and, in a turn away from Moscow, has cultivated ties with Turkey.

Tajikistan is the smallest and poorest of the Central Asian States. It suffered through a protracted civil war in the 1990s that drained the resources of already strained public institutions. Though a negotiated peace was put into effect, the conflicts, especially between Muslim fundamentalists and those who prefer a secular government, threatened the development of the country. There are also frequent armed conflicts with drug traffickers from neighboring Afghanistan.

Kazakhstan president, Nursultan Nazarbayev.

INDEPENDENCE DOES NOT EQUAL DEMOCRACY

The Central Asian States had all declared "state sovereignty" a year before the breakup of the Soviet Union, which dissolved with the formation of the Commonwealth of Independent States (CIS) on December 21, 1991. The CIS is a forum for communication and cooperation similar in some ways to the European Union.

The new Central Asian States were essentially on their own after centuries of conquest and colonialism. According to scholar Gregory Gleason, the only way the new countries could avoid chaos was to rely as much as possible on existing institutions and the people who ran them:

In the absence of general principles to guide the process of transition, politics took precedence over principles. The urgent and the necessary took precedence over the

THE JEWS OF CENTRAL ASIA

Because of the often violent conflicts between Jews and Muslims in the Middle East and because the Central Asian States are predominantly Muslim, many assume that there are no Jews in the region. But in fact, Jews have lived in Central Asia for centuries, generally getting along well with the Muslim majority. An exception was during the Soviet era, when all religious expression was discouraged, though even then Jews were able to practice their faith openly in more remote areas of Soviet Central Asia.

Americans Hershel Shanks and Suzanne Singer visited Central Asia in 1998 to find out how the Jews were getting along in the newly independent nations. In an October 1998 article titled "Oil and Jews on the Silk Road," published in *Moment* magazine, Shanks and Singer reported that

> Historically, [Muslim] relations with their long-time Jewish communities have been, by and large, not simply tolerant, but often cordial. That is certainly true today. . . . At a luncheon for Jewish war veterans in Tashkent, the non-Jewish "mayor" of the . . . quarter of the city in which it was held spoke warmly of the Jewish contribution to their society, urging the Jewish community to remain in Uzbekistan.

Shanks and Singer recounted an incident that illustrated for them how successfully the Jews of Central Asia had adapted to conditions both before and after the collapse of the Soviet Union:

> We were standing at the reception desk of our hotel in Samarkand, asking for directions to the synagogue in the old city. Two well-dressed guests offered to help. It turned out that they had been born in Samarkand and had come back for a visit, perhaps to show off their new-found wealth. They owned a photo shop in Moscow. Their business card, with a full-color picture, indicated that "Royal Photo" in Moscow has four telephone lines and a fax. They graciously offered the services of their driver to take us to the synagogue. We mumbled something about their kindness. "*Ain ba'aya*," they responded in Hebrew. "No problem." That is how we learned they were Jews. That they had moved to Moscow and opened a business is only one point of this story. A second: There was no reluctance on the part of these Jews to speak Hebrew in the hotel lobby of this former Soviet republic.

beneficial and the desired. Since the former communist leaders of Central Asia commanded the only institutions capable of guiding the process of . . . dismantling . . . the state-run economies and Communist Party–dominated political system—these communist leaders themselves assumed responsibility for engineering the transition to postcommunist rule.[5]

Many in the West thought that as soon as the repressive Soviet system ended in Central Asia, democracy would flourish. The assumption was that all people see the advantages of democracy, want it, and are willing to fight—or at least protest—to get it. In fact, the trend in Central Asia since the mid-1990s has been toward less democracy and tighter governmental control.

THE DECOLONIZATION OF CENTRAL ASIA

Because the Central Asian States gained their independence quickly, they lacked the national evolution that countries normally experience, which often takes decades to complete. Observers of the situation in Central Asia see the process the new nations went through in the 1990s as similar to what happened to many countries in the twentieth century as they gained their independence. The process is known as decolonization, meaning that a nation once ruled by a stronger country must now fend for itself. The national boundaries of the Central Asian States were artifically drawn by the Soviets in the 1920s. The boundaries were set with little regard for the distribution of ethnic groups, and tension between these groups erupts as they try to determine national policy. Thus, ethnic conflict in Central Asia has often impeded economic and political reform. This is most apparent in the Fergana Valley, where disputes over land and water management are common.

When African colonies became independent between 1957 and 1967, popular movements had advocated independence, so their leaders were ready to take on the responsibility of governing. In Central Asia, however, there were essentially no such movements and hence an extreme leadership vacuum. In the Central Asian States, few people had studied approaches to government and policy making (especially foreign policy) different from the approach endorsed by

WAR HORSES

In the Soviet era, horse breeding and training in Turkmenistan was put under state control and, in the opinion of many, almost ruined. Since independence, however, there has been a revival among Turkmen horse enthusiasts and entrepreneurs. In his book *Sacred Horses: Memoirs of a Turkmen Cowboy*, American author Jonathon Maslow explains why the horse has been central to life and politics in Central Asia for centuries.

By profession the Turkmen was a mercenary for the local despots. Agriculture was secondary. In times of peace between the khans, the Turkmen continued as warriors on their own account, organizing raids against other settlements. Their one recreation was, of course, horseracing. In this Spartan military existence, they were indissolubly bound to their horses, which were always hand fed, watered daily, covered in felt blankets against the summer sun and winter cold, and kept tethered winter and summer on a long rope outside the Turkmen's *kibitka*. Whether fighting or racing, the Turkmen showered all his affection and attention on his horse, trained it himself according to precise customs, and prepared his sons to continue the equestrian tradition. From the time they were two years old, the children were made to grip boulders between their legs to develop their riding muscles. The great expanse of the Kara Kum Desert lying to the north and east ensured that no infiltration of northern horse types could occur from Mongolia and Kazakhstan. No Turkmen would adulterate the tribal stock with genes of the smaller, shaggier, phlegmatic Mongolian horses, which were considered inferior in every way. Hadn't the great Genghis Khan himself conquered the khanates of Khiva, Bukhara, and Merv to obtain tribute in what the Chinese called the horse of heaven?

With the Russian takeover of Turkestan in the 1880s, however, the mercenary armies were disbanded and the first attempts were made to settle the nomads. The economic and social base for horse breeding began to disappear. Rather than lose their most cherished traditions, many Turkmen moved their tents and horses farther into the desert, or to eastern Iran, Turkey, and Afghanistan, where more than a million Turkmen reside to this day.

the Soviet system. Even the idea of nationhood was discouraged under the Soviet system, which saw itself as transitional, to be replaced someday by a one-world Communist government.

The first decade of decolonization in Central Asia was often profoundly disappointing, characterized by retreats from democracy, a crumbling agricultural and industrial infrastructure, fewer and less effective public services, and inattention to the development of such necessities of modern life as electrical generation, communications, transport systems, and public health. One expert recently cited Central Asia as the region of the world in which there has been the greatest deterioration in public health services in the recent past, and she warns that this can have severe consequences for the future.

GROWING PAINS

When the Central Asian States went from being under central control from Moscow to being independent governments, they were acutely in need of help, but no one had

During the first decade of Central Asia's independence, a crumbling infrastructure and lack of leadership led to a deterioration in public health services.

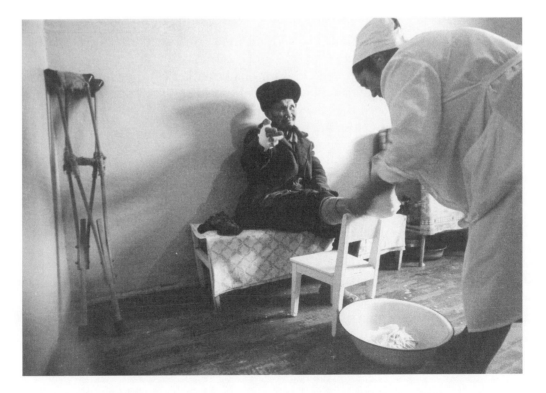

been trained in how to relate to other governments. They had been taught to think that Western organizations like the International Monetary Fund and the World Bank were tools of the capitalist system, but now these were the very organizations they had to ask for help with their economic problems and ecological disasters. The new governments found that they were often most effective when they banded together to solve problems, but at the same time, banding together forced each nation to compromise and defer some of its own interests.

Since independence, the Central Asian States have made only halting and clumsy attempts at reform and have tended to stifle rather than tolerate dissent and change. Uzbekistan is a case in point. Some Uzbeks have called for a bigger role for Islam in public affairs. Those in power, however, see some forms of Islam as a threat. They fear an Islamic revolution like those in Iran in the late 1970s and in Afghanistan in the 1990s. The government's response has been to ban many forms of Islamic practice. Instead of quieting the situation, the result has been an increase in Islamic militancy and cries of protest from international human rights organizations. And in trying to control the Uzbek economy by monetary and trade restrictions, the government has made it harder for people to start and run legitimate businesses, leading to an upsurge in both black-market commerce and corrupt practices like bribery and money laundering. Thus, in general the government's attempts to control situations have been self-defeating.

EXPERIMENTS IN DEMOCRACY

Democracy is not a new idea, but it is a new reality for many nations. It is not surprising that the new Central Asian States have had many difficulties in moving toward democracy. For example, Kazakhstan and Turkmenistan both became one-party states in the late 1990s, meaning that those who opposed the government were denied the right to organize into political parties.

In the early 1990s, many in the West thought that Kyrgyzstan was the country where democracy was most likely to flourish. The country's parliament had selected Askar Akayev, a physicist and head of the Kyrgyz Academy of Sciences, as its first president, and then he was reelected twice by popular vote. Western analysts thought that having a president who had not been a former Communist Party boss would mean Kyrgyzstan would be the bright spot in Central Asia. In some ways that has been true. President Akayev's initial reforms were the most sweeping in the region, and he spoke eloquently of his hopes for his country's future:

> The idea of "Kyrgyzstan—our common home" has become the recognized basis for enhancing and strengthening inter-ethnic harmony and creating the conditions for a life in dignity for all citizens of the country. In Kyrgyzstan, which has absorbed in equal measure the spiritual heritage and rich traditions of the East and the West, representatives of many ethnic groups and religious faiths live together in peace and harmony.[6]

Though the Kyrgyz constitution allows presidents to serve only two terms, Akayev announced that he would ignore the constitution and run again. As the 2000 elections approached, it seemed that Akayev might have a formidable opponent, Felix Kulov, a former close associate of Akayev's who had served in several government posts. Kulov had become popular in 1990 when he was the interior minister and helped to diffuse ethnic tensions.

Kulov announced that he would run for president on March 22, 2000, and was immediately arrested on charges related to his tenure as security minister in 1994. After arresting Kulov, Akayev's government took other measures to stifle dissent. It shut down the newspaper *Res Publica* (Public Affairs) and fined its editors several thousand dollars for having published a letter critical of a government official. Other journalists have been arrested and tried on what government critics see as false charges, even though Kyrgyz law guarantees freedom of the press. And despite laws mandating fair and open trials, Kulov's trial in August 2000 was closed to the press and public.

To the surprise of many, Kulov was acquitted. Western political analysts and human rights activists think that the verdict may have been due more to the courage of the judge than to a change in policy by the government. The Kulov case illustrates several aspects of political life in Central Asia at the end of the first decade of independence: Even though the

A Kyrgyzstan woman votes in her country's 2000 parliamentary elections as election workers (left) keep track of turnout and a police officer watches in the background.

nations have constitutions and laws that read very much like those in the West, they can be bent or broken by authorities, and the leaders of the new nations are entrenched in office and willing to use their power to suppress political opposition. On the other hand, the arrest and trial of Felix Kulov generated worldwide media attention, and this may have emboldened both Kyrgyz protesters and the judge.

But the drama was not over. After his acquittal, Kulov said he needed time to decide whether to run for president. Then the election commission announced that all candidates would have to pass an exam testing their command of Kyrgyz, based on a clause of the constitution requiring candidates for president to be proficient in the state language. However, the constitution also says that no one can be denied political rights based on lack of proficiency in Kyrgyz, and no language test had been given to candidates prior to the 1990 and 1995 elections. This led to charges that the election commission was trying to exclude candidates, especially Felix Kulov, whose principal language is Russian. And amid growing signs of Kulov's popularity, the court that acquitted him in August announced in September that it was reviewing its decision, raising the possibility that he could be imprisoned after all. Kulov, however, refused to take the language test and threw his support to another candidate.

The Kulov case makes clear that while the fight for democracy in Central Asia is far from over, in the coming years those in power may have to treat the opposition more fairly or face a torrent of bad publicity.

FORMING NATIONAL IDENTITIES

The process of independence turned the political landscape upside down. Ideas considered dangerous under the Soviet system, like ethnic pride, nationalism, and the promotion of local cultures, were now politically advantageous. According to Gleason,

Many political leaders in Central Asia shifted their stance on key "nationalist" issues. They quickly became champions of local languages as official government languages. [President Islam] Karimov in Uzbekistan (who spoke Uzbek only haltingly before independence) took intensive training in the native tongue. He quickly and successfully learned to make speeches in Uzbek rather than Russian. The Central Asian leaders repositioned themselves as champions of the historical and cultural legacies of Central Asia. Having earlier condemned the nationalist opposition as politically naïve, foreign-inspired and -financed, and antagonistic to the interests of the people and the republic, the leaders quickly attempted to buy off the most talented members of the opposition by offering them key jobs within the government. In this way, the sentiment of the opposition movements ended up, ironically, strengthening the new states of Central Asia.[7]

However, because the states all have multiple ethnic groups, there has not

To show his support for nationalist issues, Uzbekistan president Islam Karimov quickly learned and made speeches in Uzbek rather than Russian.

been complete agreement about how to accommodate minority rights and interests. In Uzbekistan, the Karakalpak minority has an autonomous region, meaning that in most respects they are in charge of their own affairs while remaining part of Uzbekistan, an arrangement somewhat like Indian reservations in the United States. But in the Fergana Valley, where many ethnic Uzbeks live in Kyrgyzstan and Tajikistan, solutions have been harder to find. According to an August 2000 article by reporter Joseph Fritchett, Fergana

> has fallen prey to decay and unrest, starting with quarrels between governments and, often just as dangerous, fractious tribal groups. Roads that carried farm produce to markets have been cut by border crossings and even more numerous armed check points designed to protect minorities from each other. A Western diplomat in Tashkent explained, "People are fighting for jobs, housing, even food, so they revert to their ethnic and tribal bases.[8]

THE STATUS OF THE RUSSIANS

Since independence, ethnic Russians have been concerned about their status in the new nations. During the Soviet era they were encouraged to move to Central Asia to run the government, industrial plants, and agriculture. They tended to keep to themselves, not socializing much with the native people, many of whom saw the Russians as oppressors. Likewise, the Russians tended to see their assignments in Central Asia as unpleasant and longed to return to Russia.

But when the Soviet Union dissolved, the situation for the Russians became even more complicated and difficult. Russia was in turmoil, and the chances of finding work there were slim. Nevertheless, many returned to Russia. Others, however, have stayed in Central Asia, fearing that conditions back home would be even worse. As Gregory Gleason states,

> The creation of the independent states has exacerbated many of the social problems left over from the Soviet period. Central Asia's agricultural specialization created ethnic stratification as a result of a cultural division of labor. [That is, Russians had higher-status jobs than those of the native ethnic groups.] Since independence, the promises of social support, health services, guaran-

teed incomes, and other elements of "welfare authoritarianism" have come to be little more than that—promises. Corruption and organized crime continue to be pervasive and endemic problems in all of the Central Asian countries. And the large numbers of people of Slavic [Russian, for example] and nonindigenous nationalities who remain in Central Asia . . . are concerned about the protection of their civil rights and their new status as "second-class citizens" of the states. Many, of course, voted with their feet and returned to Russia or other parts of the former Soviet Union, but many have not found that to be practical or have remained in Central Asia.[9]

ECONOMIC INTERDEPENDENCE

During the Soviet era, there was no question of economic cooperation: Everything was coordinated by the government in Moscow. Though this stifled innovation and resulted in some spectacular environmental disasters, it ensured that the basic sorts of cooperation needed among five administrations all in the same geographic region took place. After independence, it was less clear how decisions should be made and how the five new nations would work together to maintain economic relations.

The Central Asian States have tended to follow the models for cooperation that have been successful in other regions of the world. For example, Kazakhstan, Kyrgyzstan, Tajikistan, Belarus, and Russia have formed the Commonwealth of Independent States Customs Union to make it easier to move merchandise across borders. Since 1997 Kazakhstan, Kyrgyzstan, Tajikistan, and Uzbekistan have been members of the Central Asia Economic Community, whose goals are greater cooperation in the development of the regional economies. And in 1998, Kyrgyzstan became the first of the Central Asian States to join the World Trade Organization, which sets standards for international trade and settles disputes among member nations.

The CIS originally aimed to create a common economic market and a single currency for the region, much like the European Union's euro, which is gradually replacing the currencies of the nations of Europe. But by 2000, a single currency for the Central Asian States seemed unlikely because of

Kazakh president Nursultan Nazarbayev (second from right) gestures as his counterparts in the Central Asian Economic Community, (from left to right) Tajikistan's Imomali Rakhmonov, Uzbekistan's Islam Karimov, and Kyrgyzstan's Askar Akayev, look on.

increased nationalist feelings, major internal political problems, autocratic governments unwilling to give up control, and economies that at best were limping into the twenty-first century.

NATIONAL DEFENSE

An important aspect of the CIS is defense coordination. Kyrgyzstan, Tajikistan, and Turkmenistan have southern neighbors—Iran and Afghanistan—with severe internal conflicts that have sometimes erupted into violence. The armies of the Central Asian States are very dependent on Russia for weapons, supplies, training, and advice, a situation that the United States has had to accept as the only way to bring stability to the region.

The issue that has been of greatest concern to the international community has been the nuclear arsenal of the former Soviet Union. Kazakhstan was the site of the Semipalatinsk nuclear weapons test facility, one of the largest in the world, where 150 above-ground nuclear tests were conducted between 1949 and 1962. Hundreds more underground tests were performed there before the collapse of the USSR. In November 1994, the United States learned that there were six hundred pounds of plutonium (a necessary component of nuclear weapons) in Kazakhstan that were in danger of being sold to Iran, which had sent out teams of officials to try to buy nuclear materials from the former Soviet republics. With the cooperation of Russia, the United States bought the plutonium for about $10 million, sent in a military transport plane, and flew the plutonium to a U.S. facility.

In addition to having the Semipalatinsk testing facility, Kazakhstan was the only nation of the Central Asian States that had intercontinental missiles armed with nuclear weapons at the time of the breakup of the Soviet Union, and officials in the United States and Western Europe feared that they might detonate accidentally due to poor maintenance or that they might be sold to hostile nations like Iran, Iraq, or Libya. There was even fear that terrorist organizations might try to steal the bombs. The United States pledged $133 million to help dismantle Kazakhstan's nuclear weapons, and by March 1995 there were none left in the country.

RELATIONS WITH CHINA

Eugene Romer of the U.S. National Defense University has said that the greatest foreign policy concern of Central Asian leaders is China. When Romer visited Central Asia in the fall of 1999, he and other U.S. experts made a presentation to senior politicians about various foreign policy issues. Romer recalls that

> The locals looked bored as [we] went on about presidential succession in Russia, Gov. George W. Bush's foreign policy, and Europe after the Kosovo war. But the half-dozen men snapped to attention when China came up. China was what worried them most and what they understood least. Living next to China has proved difficult. . . . Despite their extensive common border, [the Central Asian States] had virtually no experience dealing with it prior to 1991. During the Soviet period, the relationship with Beijing was managed in Moscow. Confronted with a giant, nontransparent, dogmatic neighbor with great power ambitions, the young states of Central Asia knew they'd have a hard time dealing with it on their own.[10]

THE CENTRAL ASIAN TEA CEREMONY

The tea ceremony is very important to Central Asians. Tea drinkers traditionally sit on a carpet at a low table. Tea is served in a small cup with no handles called a *piala*. After pouring the first cup from a fresh pot, the host will return the tea twice to the pot before serving it to the guest of honor. The guests place their left hand over their heart and accept their cup with their right hand. Tea that is too hot is cooled by swirling it gently in the cup, never by blowing. If the tea becomes cold, the host will throw it out and refill the cup. Filling a cup to the brim is a sign that the host wishes his guest to leave quickly; a cup filled only partway, on the other hand, is an invitation to stay for many refills.

A Turkman pours tea into a piala *during a traditional tea ceremony.*

The solution that the Central Asian States have adopted is engagement with China over the issue the Chinese are most worried about: calls for independence by Central Asian ethnic minorities living in western China. When the Central Asian States became independent, China feared that they might help dissidents incite a violent revolution. Although protests and violence by ethnic minorities in western China have increased in recent years, the Central Asian States have been careful not to aid them and have entered into several agreements with the Chinese to combat the "terrorism and drug trafficking" that have been linked to the nationalist movements the Chinese want to suppress.

Dealing with China was similar to the other challenges the Central Asian States faced during their first ten years of independence. In addition to forming relations with regional powers like Russia and Iran, the region faced environmental collapse, economic stagnation, and political instability. Scholars fear that the traditional hierarchical cultures of the region, the legacy of Soviet authoritarianism and mismanagement, and the lack of legal and financial structures to encourage investment mean that it may be a long time before Central Asia is able to reach its full potential.

4

DAILY LIFE IN CENTRAL ASIA

A visitor to Central Asia will be struck almost immediately with extreme contrasts between the modern and the ancient. In a single day you can see new international airports and desert oases that have been in continuous use for thousands of years; gleaming steel and glass office buildings and ancient stone fortresses; a surveying crew scouting routes for an oil pipeline and a camel caravan bringing wool down from a mountain sheep station. You might see a group of *aq saqal*, or "gray beards," older men who are looked to for advice and wisdom, sitting in the shade of a tree discussing the affairs of their community over tea—a custom at least a thousand years old—when one of them excuses himself to answer his cell phone. Contact with the outside world increases daily in the newly independent states of Central Asia. As the peoples, cultures, and technologies of Asia, Europe, the Middle East, and America become more important and influential, the people of Central Asia search for ways to retain, and sometimes to recover, their distinctive ways of life.

AN OPPRESSED MAJORITY

Although no ethnic group is in the majority in Central Asia, there is one clear majority: 52 percent of the population are women, meaning that there are roughly 2 million more females than males in the region. Women have equal status under the new constitutions, but they have little political power and their career opportunities are often limited. The Soviet-era "equality" of women—which often meant that women studied and worked alongside men while still retaining their homemaking chores—has reverted to more traditional values that favor early marriage and large families. Daily life for the majority of Central Asians, then, is controlled by the sex-role customs of the native cultures. Impor-

tant factors in how strictly traditional customs are followed are the educational level of the family and whether the family is urban or rural (better-educated urban families tend to be more flexible).

Some aspects of life for girls and women are similar to what is common in the United States and Europe. For example, general education is compulsory for both sexes, and some Islamic schools are coeducational. Women can go to universities and technical schools, but they are less likely than their Western counterparts to receive proper preparation for professional careers and get the support of their families. Women are still not admitted to *madrasahs*, which are schools for the advanced study of Islam.

Many aspects of daily life for Central Asian women remind them of their status as second-class citizens. For example, the bride price, money given in exchange for a woman's hand in marriage, is still common in Tajikistan and Turkmenistan. Central Asian women tend not to lead conversations or shake hands. They do not drink in public. They are not allowed to enter working mosques. Men tend not to address

While women in Central Asia receive general education, career opportunities are often limited. These women make their living selling fruit along an Uzbekistan road.

ETIQUETTE IN CENTRAL ASIA

Muslims consider the left hand unclean and eat only with the right. They do not point the sole of their shoes or feet at others, nor do they step over any part of another person's body or walk in front of someone praying to Mecca. People remove their shoes before entering a home or a mosque, and dirty socks or shoes are considered an insult. Central Asians would never think of putting their feet up on a table, or near any food that is spread on a cloth on the floor. Blowing one's nose in public, common practice in the United States, is considered disgusting in Central Asia.

Central Asian etiquette mandates the removal of one's shoes before entering a mosque.

women directly, speaking instead to their male companions, because "it is regarded as impolite to speak to another man's wife."[11] In Tajikistan, conditions for women are especially poor. According to one scholar, "in the last decades of the twentieth century, Tajik social norms and even de facto government policy still often favored a traditionalist, restrictive attitude toward women that tolerated wife beating and the arbitrary dismissal of women from responsible positions."[12]

However, in Kyrgyzstan women play a more prominent public role than elsewhere in Central Asia, holding many key posts in government and the private sector. In the decade after independence, Kyrgyz women served as the minister of education, state procurator (the top law enforcement official), ambassador to the United States and Canada, and minister of foreign affairs. Roza Otunbayeva, a former minister of foreign affairs, was mentioned frequently as a possible successor to Askar Akayev as president of Kyrgyzstan.

HOME LIFE

Traditional households in Central Asia separate the sexes, with women spending their time in the kitchen and perhaps an attached patio and men in the living room and dining room areas or outside on a covered porch or under a shade tree. The degree to which families follow this tradition varies. For example, American writer Jonathon Maslow visited Turkmenistan in the late 1980s and found that his host family, in which both husband and wife were physicians, practiced this separation of the sexes but were not very strict about it.

WOMEN'S SAVINGS PARTIES

Uzbeks do not have a great deal of trust in their national banks, which tend to be corrupt. Consequently, Uzbeks do not put their money aside into savings accounts. But Uzbek women use a time-honored and well-respected alternative to save their money—monthly saving parties. At the party, each woman contributes two weeks' pay, and the total amount is awarded to a different woman each month. In a July 2000 field report titled "Women's Savings Parties in Uzbekistan" (available at www.cacianalyst.org), writer Chris Aslan describes one such party held by ten women in Khiva, Uzbekistan.

All the women are connected in some way, as relatives, neighbors or friends and it is this bond of trust that makes their savings party work. After huge shared plates of rice and mutton have been dispensed with, and all the latest gossip is chewed over, each of the women hands over a bundle of notes to Gulnora [the hostess] and asks her what she will do with her savings. Gulnora had planned to buy a loom and wool with the money, but recently found an ideal match for her teenage son and will use the money to pay for the wedding. Before leaving, the women discuss who will host the party next month, and walk home dreaming of how they will use their cash bonanza of five months wages, when their turn comes around.

Housing in Central Asia is generally similar in construction to Western-style homes and apartments, but a large proportion do not have the utilities that are taken for granted in the United States, such as running water, central heating, and sewer lines. Most families—except in the most rural areas—own televisions, refrigerators, sewing machines, and washing machines. Decorations and furnishings are often of the same sort that would have been used in past centuries. According to Maslow, in his hosts' home, "The floors were spread and the walls were hung with oriental carpets. The bedding was rolled up and stored in a chest during the day, and everyone scrupulously removed their shoes before entering."[13]

Under the Soviets, housing was supplied by the government or employers, and there was a severe housing shortage. After independence, a variety of approaches were used to transfer housing to private ownership, a gradual process that remained incomplete in the late 1990s. In general, the privatization of housing meant that rents increased, and the housing crisis became even more acute. Because of the

THE YURT

The nomadic yurt (*kiizuy* in Kazakh and *bosuy* in Kyrgyz) is a round tent that can be set up or dismantled in one to four hours. Traditionally, a collapsed yurt was transported by horse, camel, or oxen. A yurt consists of a flexible willow-wood frame covered with multilayered felt (*kiyiz*) that has been coated in waterproof sheep fat. Woven woolen strips (*tizgych*) secure the framework to long poles (*uyuk*) that rise up to the apex (*shanrak*) of the yurt. An opening at the top controls temperature, allows air and light to get in, and lets smoke from the central hearth escape. The size of the opening can be increased or decreased with a flap.

The entrance to a yurt usually faces east and has a door made from a woven grass mat (*chiy*) or carved wood. The floors are covered with multicolored felt mats (*koshma*) and rugs (*shyrdaks*). The interior walls are decorated with brightly colored rugs, quilts, cushions, camel and horse bags, and large tassels. Embroidered or woven bags (*aiyk kap*) hung from the interior poles are used for storing plates and clothing. The social standing of the yurt's owners is indicated by the elaborateness of the decorations.

Two Kyrgyzstan women weave cloth on a portable loom outside of their nomadic yurt.

shortage of homes, many people lived in cramped conditions, with two or three generations of a family in a single small apartment. While people languished on waiting lists, construction of new housing decreased due to tight budgets and disputes over private land ownership.

The yurt, a large, round tent, is the traditional form of housing in Central Asia. The design of yurts evolved to meet the demands of the nomadic lifestyle; they can be easily dismantled, transported, and set up again. Although yurts were once the main form of housing in Central Asia, they are not seen as much today as in the past—except in Kyrgyzstan. Many Kyrgyz continue the tradition of nomadic pastoralism, living in yurts and following their herds of sheep, horses, or yaks. Kyrgyz families who live in Western-style homes often erect yurts to celebrate weddings and funerals. The yurt is considered such an important symbol of Kyrgyz identity, it is even featured on their flag.

CENTRAL ASIAN CUISINE

Even though the kitchens in most houses and apartments in Central Asia are not as modern as those in the West, cooking large and elaborate meals that are enjoyed by the extended family and guests is a favorite activity. Visitors to Central Asia are often warned that they will be offered huge quantities of food at frequent family banquets and that failure to eat heartily can be taken as an insult.

Several dishes are common throughout Central Asia, and there are also local specialties. Many popular dishes come to the region from other countries—Russia, China, India, Iran, the Middle East, and the Mediterranean. Noodles, rice, herbs, savory seasonings, vegetables and legumes, yogurt, and grilled meats are frequent ingredients in Central Asian foods.

The favorite meat of the region is mutton, which is very fatty. Beef, horse meat, and camel meat are also popular, though ethnic Turkmen, whose culture is built around the breeding and training of horses, do not eat horse meat. Pork is forbidden under *halal*, the Islamic dietary laws, and is found only in Russian or Chinese restaurants. Some favorite meat dishes include goat-head soup, Kazakh horse meat sausage, *shashlyk* (mutton, beef, liver, or chicken kabobs), and *plov* (a rice and meat pilaf).

Long noodles called *laghman* are served everywhere in Central Asia. They are the main ingredient in a soup—also called *laghman*—that includes fried mutton, peppers, tomatoes, and onions. *Besbarmak* is a holiday dish in Kazakhstan and Kyrgyzstan consisting of noodles topped with lamb or horse meat. Other popular soups include *shorpa* and *manpar*, both made with mutton and vegetables. Russian borscht, a soup made of beets and sometimes served with sour cream, is also popular throughout Central Asia.

Manty are steamed or fried dumplings stuffed with meat. They are served plain or with vinegar, sour cream, or butter, and are also sometimes served in soup. *Piroshki*, fried pies usually stuffed with a mixture of fat, mutton, and onions, are a popular food that came to Central Asia from Russia. They are also sometimes filled with potatoes, pumpkin, chickpeas, curd, or greens.

Nan, a flat bread found all over Asia, is a popular accompaniment to meals. *Nan* is sometimes made with onions, meat, or sheep's tail in the dough or topped with anise, poppy, or sesame seeds. *Nishalda*, a traditional dish popular during Ramadan, consists of whipped egg whites with sugar and licorice flavoring.

Tea is a very popular drink in Central Asia. The customs surrounding the preparation and drinking of tea go back for centuries. Other favorite drinks include fermented milk beverages made from cow, sheep, goat, camel, or horse milk. *Kumys* is a mildly alcoholic fermented mare's milk enjoyed by Kazakhs and Kyrgyz. *Shubat*, a fermented camel's milk, is popular with Turkmen, Kazakh, and Karakalpak nomads. *Aryan*, a popular mixture of yogurt and water, is served either salty or sweetened.

Preparing and enjoying large, elaborate meals, which often include grilled meats, noodles, and vegetables, is a favorite activity throughout Central Asia.

TRADITIONAL CLOTHING

Though cooking in Central Asia tends to follow tradition, most men and women in Central Asia wear modern, Western- or Russian-style clothing. Traditional clothing is also worn; some articles are common throughout the five nations while others are distinctive to a particular nation or people. Sandals are popular for both sexes in Central Asia. One of the most common articles of clothing for men is the *doppe*, a four-sided black skullcap embroidered in white. In Kazakhstan and Kyrgyzstan, men also wear a tall, white felt hat with black embroidery called an *ak kalpak*. The *ak kalpak* sometimes includes a tassel on top. Probably the most distinctive type of headgear for males is the Turkmen *telpek*, a large, round sheepskin hat with thick ringlets resembling dreadlocks. The *telpek* is usually black—or white for special occasions—and is worn year-round atop the *doppe*.

The traditional headgear for Turkmen is the telpek, *a large, round sheepskin hat.*

In Kazakhstan, on special occasions, women wear long dresses with stand-up collars or brightly decorated velvet waistcoats. Kazakh women also occasionally wear heavy

jewelry and fur-trimmed headdresses decorated with crane plumes. The traditional male costume is baggy trousers and shirts with a sleeveless jacket and a wool or cotton robe.

The traditional clothing for women in Kyrgyzstan is similar to that worn in Kazakhstan. Older Kyrgyz women may also wear an *elechek*, a large white turban. A woman's status is indicated by the number of times the *elechek* is wound around her head. Kyrgyz men wear long sheepskin coats and fur-trimmed hats in winter.

Traditional Tajik clothing for women is bright and colorful. They wear striped trousers and bright slippers beneath long, multicolored dresses and matching head scarves. Tajik men wear a sashed, quilted coat called a *tapan*.

Turkmen women also wear colorful trousers beneath long dresses. Their dresses tend to be dark red or maroon and are made of velvet or silk. Women's hair is always tied back and covered with a colorful scarf. Males in Turkmenistan wear long, belted coats and baggy trousers tucked into knee-high boots. They also wear a knee-length red cotton jacket called a *khalat*.

Traditional dress for Uzbek males also includes a long, quilted coat tied by a sash. Uzbek women wear brightly colored knee-length dresses over trousers, both of which are made of a sparkly cloth called *ikat*. Women wear their hair braided, with one or two braids indicating a married woman and more braids indicating a single woman.

SHOPPING

Clothing, food, and other items can be found in a wide variety of shops in Central Asia. Street bazaars have been an important means of commerce in cities and villages for centuries, and they still exist today. Wall hangings, felt rugs, carpets, silk, traditional clothing, food, and many other items are available at bazaars. One of the largest bazaars in Central Asia is the Tolkuchka Bazaar in Ashkhabad, Turkmenistan. According to the authors of *Central Asia*, the Tolkuchka Bazaar "sprawls across acres of desert on the outskirts of town, with corrals of camels and goats, avenues of red-clothed women squatting before silver jewelry, and villages of trucks from which garrulous Uzbeks hawk everything from pistachios to car parts. Whatever you want, it's sold at Tolkuchka."[14]

Broom vendors wait for customers at a street bazaar in Samarqand, Uzbekistan. While Central Asian cities have Western-style department stores, street bazaars have been an important means of commerce for centuries.

Central Asian cities also have Western-style department stores and supermarkets. One department store, commonly known by its Russian name, TsUM, operates in Almaty and Bishkek. The central department store in Samarqand is GUM, also a survivor of the Soviet era, and in Dushanbe the department store is called Univermag. Items such as electronics, clothing, crafts, cassettes, and candy are sold at these stores. Larger cities also have supermarkets, where Central Asians can purchase many different types of food and other items similar to what is available in supermarkets in the West.

EARNING A LIVING

Following independence, Central Asia experienced many economic difficulties. Many people in rural areas were barely able to afford adequate food, and the situation in the cities was not much better. Factory managers in Bishkek earn the equivalent of eighty U.S. dollars a month, while factory workers earn only thirty-five to fifty dollars a month. Many people in Tashkent have less than five dollars a week available for food, and earn as little as twenty-five to thirty-five dollars a month. Pensions have become worthless; Kazakhstan alone owes more than $800 million in back wages and pensions. This has led to financial crisis for a number of elderly people, who sometimes must resort to begging in order to survive.

Agriculture, forestry, industry, and construction are the main occupations in Central Asia. The main form of capitalism is the so-called kiosk economy, which consists of "small-time dealers buying goods (mostly cigarettes, sweets, alcohol, cheap Chinese, Iranian and Russian clothes and furnishings) and reselling them at a higher price."[15] The authors of *Central Asia* point out that the region contains enough skilled and entrepreneurial young people to create small manufacturing enterprises that could help round out the economy, but obstacles such as bureaucracy and the unwillingness of banks to make long-term loans have thwarted such efforts.

TRANSPORTATION

Travel in Central Asia is often difficult, and making it easier is one of the largest tasks facing the new nations. Most of the highways and railway lines in Central Asia were built by the Soviets, and some are badly in need of repair. Following independence, there was also a shortage of spare parts to repair trucks, buses, and railway cars. As a result, transportation tends to be slow due to frequent breakdowns and the difficulty in obtaining parts. Though the main highways between big cities and capitals are well maintained, other roads suffer from a lack of upkeep. In addition, mountain roads are often blocked by snow in winter and landslides in the spring. This leads to many difficulties for travelers in the chiefly mountainous countries of Kyrgyzstan and Tajikistan.

Because train travel is the cheapest mode of transportation in Central Asia, trains are usually crowded. Buses are used extensively by traders to transport goods, making bus travel a cramped experience as passengers "gradually become surrounded by boxes, bags, urns and live animals."[16] Bus travel also tends to be very slow because buses must make frequent maintenance stops, and most bus service between nations has been cut.

Transportation in Kazakhstan tends to be difficult because of the great distances between the main population centers, the inhospitable terrain, and shortages of spare parts and road maintenance equipment. Only the largest cities are linked by highways. Kazakhstan Railways is the third largest rail system in the former Soviet Union, but it suffers from a lack of spare parts. Kazakhstan has two inland waterways, the Syr River in the south-central region and the Irtysh River in the northeast. Together, these rivers have a total of 2,480 miles of navigable waterway. There are ports on the Caspian Sea at Fort Shevchenko and the cities of Aqtaū and Atyraū.

The two main population centers of Kyrgyzstan, Bishkek in the north and Osh in the south, are separated by mountains that effectively divide the country in two. Transportation between these two regions is made difficult by the mountain terrain, sparse population, and fuel shortages (Kyrgyzstan has to import all its gasoline). Kyrgyzstan's road and railroad systems in the north are connected to Kazakhstan, and the transportation networks in the south are connected to Uzbekistan—making transportation to neighboring nations easier than traveling through Kyrgyzstan itself. There are two international airports in Kyrgyzstan, but a shortage of jet fuel means that Kyrgyz often must rely on the Almaty airport in Kazakhstan. Kyrgyzstan has no inland waterways.

There are no international airports or inland waterways in Tajikistan, and the few highways are of poor quality. Like Kyrgyzstan, the north and south are separated by mountains that make transportation between the two regions difficult. There is only one major highway, linking Dushanbe in the southwest with Khudzhand in the northwest, 186 miles away. This highway goes through the mountains and is frequently blocked by snow, avalanches, and landslides. The railroad is the most important means of transportation in Tajikistan, but most railway lines link the northern and southern regions with neighboring countries rather than with each other. In addition, because of the jigsaw-puzzle borders set by the Soviet Union in the 1920s, rail traffic between the northern and southern regions has to go through Uzbekistan. After independence, problems with substandard equipment decreased both passenger and freight service, and delivery of goods to remote regions became unpredictable.

Although there are no navigable rivers in Turkmenistan, there are ports along the Caspian Sea, the largest of which is at Turkmenbashy. One major highway, the Turkmenbashy-

A train, linking Uzbekistan and the Urals, travels at the base of the Tian Shan Mountains.

Ashkhabad-Chärjew Highway, connects the eastern and western population centers. There is a need for an upgraded and expanded highway system, especially "in the mountains and deserts of the republic, where only camels provide an alternate means of transport."[17] The railroad system was built by the Russians in the 1880s and is badly outdated.

In Uzbekistan, the Amu River is the main waterway, but low water levels have reduced steamship travel. An extensive railroad system in Uzbekistan connects all parts of the country and is used primarily for freight transport. The Transcaspian Railroad, the main line, connects Tashkent with the Amu River, Bukhara, and Samarqand. Uzbekistan has the most extensive road network of all the Central Asian nations. There are three major highways: the Great Uzbek Highway, which connects Tashkent to Termiz; the Zarafshon Highway, which connects Samarqand to Chärjew in Turkmenistan; and a connecter road between Tashkent and Qŭqon. Two-thirds of all passenger traffic in Uzbekistan is by bus. The capital, Tashkent, has a subway system that was designed as a nuclear shelter. Tashkent's Yuzhnyy Airport is Central Asia's main international airport, with links to Asia, Europe, and the United States.

Each of the Central Asian States has a national airline, but of these only Uzbekistan Airways remained in compliance with international air safety standards during the 1990s. Tajikistan International Airlines was nearing collapse after the country's long civil war. Kazakhstan, Kyrgyzstan, Turkmenistan, and Uzbekistan have international airports. According to the book *Central Asia*, "Flights between the biggest cities generally stick to their schedules, but those serving smaller towns are often delayed without explanation and cancellations are common, usually a result of fuel shortages."[18]

EDUCATION

General education is compulsory in Central Asia from about age six to sixteen, although some nations have lowered the number of mandatory school years. Children begin their public schooling with preschool or kindergarten, then go on to primary school and secondary school. Many join the workforce after completing ninth or tenth grade. Others leave secondary school earlier to enter trade or technical schools or universities. Nearly 100 percent of the population is literate.

There have been education reforms in the five nations since independence, with increased emphasis on Central Asian history and literature. One issue that remains unresolved is what the language of instruction should be—Russian or the native language. This issue is especially thorny in Kazakhstan, where ethnic Russians and Ukrainians make up more than 50 percent of the population.

Another problem has been the shifting of alphabets from Arabic to Roman to Cyrillic during the twentieth century. Some nations returned to Roman after independence. This has presented a peculiar situation of older generations using alphabets that are incomprehensible to younger generations.

All five nations have had to cut back their budgets for education. School buildings are in poor repair, and there is not enough money to construct new facilities. As a result, many schools are crowded. There is also a shortage of paper and other supplies and equipment. In addition, teachers are poorly paid—or sometimes not paid—and have heavy teaching loads. This has led to many teachers switching to higher-paying jobs.

At the turn of the twenty-first century, textbooks were in short supply. Soviet-era textbooks were still used in some schools but were outdated and politically irrelevant. In some parts of Central Asia, attempts to eradicate old-style Soviet textbooks left shelves empty. In Uzbekistan, textbooks containing references to the country's Communist past were removed from schools, and the newly independent nations could not afford to print their own textbooks.

About 10 percent of Central Asians have some form of higher education. The university degree system used in the United States was adopted in 1992. Courses of study are available in medicine, veterinary studies, agriculture, business, economics, music, theater, foreign language, industry, auto repair, road building, architecture, and a variety of engineering and technical fields. Higher education is hindered by a shortage of labs, libraries, computers, and facilities to publish and distribute research findings.

Students raise their hands during a lesson in ethnic tolerance in a Kyrgyz language school.

Some nations have reclassified secondary technical schools as universities. Kyrgyzstan, in response to the number of Russian-speaking students leaving the country to obtain higher education, created the Slavic University in 1992 in order to provide a Russian-language institution for students from all over Central Asia. Many Kyrgyz have criticized the new university, however, saying that the country's limited education funds should go to the education of Kyrgyz students.

Since independence, the five Central Asian States have begun to make their own choices about how to budget their money, and there has been a trend away from funding for education. The situation continues to be in flux.

HEALTH CARE

There have also been cutbacks in health care. Under Soviet rule, the five Central Asian republics had the same access to free basic health care as all the other Soviet socialist republics did. Free health care continued to be offered in Central Asia in the decade following independence, but budget cutbacks in each of the nations made it difficult to maintain the standards in the health care system that existed before independence. And each of the Central Asian nations has been unable to afford adequate quantities of basic medical supplies such as drugs, vaccines, and syringes, which previously had been imported from Russia and Finland. Medical and pharmaceutical research also suffered cutbacks. Most hospitals and clinics were overcrowded, underequipped, sometimes unsanitary, and understaffed, and many medical personnel were poorly trained. In some rural areas they did not even have running water, and there were no funds for construction of new facilities. Doctors were poorly paid or sometimes not paid at all, and in most of Central Asia they were not allowed to open a private practice. As a consequence of the low pay, many health care professionals switched to higher-paying jobs in other professions or left Central Asia altogether. A large proportion were from Russia and emigrated back after independence.

Because the public health care system is inadequate, the Central Asian States are looking for alternatives. Plans for the development of public health insurance and privatization of health care facilities are under way in most of Central Asia. In Turkmenistan, many people have returned to more traditional means of medical care from healers who use herbs and prayer.

Unfortunately, the health care system has been inadequate to deal with the numerous health issues that have appeared as a result of the severe environmental problems left from the Soviet era such as pesticide and herbicide contamination from agriculture and nuclear fallout from weapons tests. Many diseases that were formerly eradicated or controlled have returned, such as typhoid, paratyphoid, hepatitis (from contaminated drinking water), diphtheria, cholera, dysentery, brucellosis, anthrax, and tick-borne hemorrhagic fever. Most of Central Asia has seen a sharp increase in tuberculosis. Several cases of bubonic plague have occurred in Kazakhstan, where in 1995 "a bubonic plague–carrying rat population was moving from the Balkhash region [in Kazakhstan], where the plague is endemic, southward toward Almaty, whose municipal government had taken no measures to control rats."[19] In 1999 further outbreaks of bubonic plague occurred in the Kazakh cities of Aqtaū and Qyzylorda.

PUBLIC HOLIDAYS AND HOLY DAYS

Soviet-era restrictions on Islam have been lifted, and religious holidays have seen a resurgence in Central Asia since independence. Kazakhstan is the only Central Asian nation in which the government does not allow Islamic holy days to be public holidays; however, it does allow the Muslim spring festival (*Navrus*) and summer festival (*Kymyzuryndyk*), both of which have pre-Islamic roots, as public holidays.

Banks, businesses, and government offices are closed in Central Asia on public holidays. All five nations observe New Year's Day (January 1), International Women's Day (March 8), *Navrus* (around March 21), and Labor Day (May 1). In addition, each of the five nations celebrates its own Independence Day, and some celebrate their own Constitution Day.

The biggest Central Asian holiday is *Navrus*, celebrated on the spring equinox. The Muslim holiday was banned by the Soviets, but the ban was lifted in 1989. Today *Navrus* is celebrated as a two-day festival with bonfires, poetry recitals, music, games, and street art. Traditional food is prepared, including *sumalakh*, a wheat dish for women, and *khalem*, a beef dish for men. Also included in the ceremony are wine, milk, sweets, sugar, sherbet, candles, and a new flower bud.

Uzbek dancers perform during the holiday of Navrus, *celebrated throughout Central Asia on the spring equinox.*

Muslim holy days are observed in Kyrgyzstan, Tajikistan, Turkmenistan, and Uzbekistan. The Muslim calendar consists of lunar months, which begin at the new moon, so dates of holy days change each year in relationship to the Western calendar. Ramadan, the month of fasting from sunrise to sunset, is celebrated each year. *Eid-ul-Fitr* is a two- or three-day celebration at the end of Ramadan consisting of family visits, banquets, and donations to the poor. *Eid-ul-Azha* is the Feast of Sacrifice, celebrated over several days in February or March. It involves the slaughtering of an animal to share with family and the poor. *Mawlid-an-Nabi,* the birthday of the prophet Muhammad, is celebrated in May or June each year.

SPORTS AND RECREATION

Horses have played an important role in defining Central Asian culture, so it is no surprise that the most popular forms of recreation and sporting events are equestrian. One of the most popular sports is a game called *buzkashi*, which is played on horseback. Bradley Mayhew and his coauthors describe the game in their book *Central Asia:*

As close to warfare as a sport can get, buzkashi is a bit like rugby on horseback in which the "ball" is the headless carcass of a calf, goat or sheep (whatever is handy).

The day before the kick-off the carcass (or *boz*) has its head, lower legs and entrails removed and is soaked in cold water for 24 hours to toughen it up. The game begins with the carcass in the center of a circle at one end of a field; at the other end is a bunch of wild, adrenaline-crazed horsemen. At a signal it's every man for himself as they charge for the carcass. The aim is to gain possession of the boz and carry it up to the field and around a post, with the winning rider being the one who finally drops the boz back in the circle. All the while there's a frenzied horse-backed tug-of-war going on as each competitor tries to gain possession; smashed noses, wrenched shoulders and shattered thigh bones are all part of the fun.[20]

Kyrgyz villagers jostle each other during an equestrian sporting event.

Another popular equestrian game involves a man on horseback chasing a woman and trying to kiss her. This game began as an alternative to abduction—the traditional nomadic way to take a wife. Horse racing, horseback archery, horseback wrestling, polo, and eagle-hunting contests are also popular. Other popular sports include wrestling, soccer, and baseball.

The sports of the Central Asian States are like other aspects of daily life there: a study in contrasts between the old and the new. The people of Central Asia are struggling to find ways to retain their traditional ways and still become part of the modern world. Despite formidable obstacles, in many ways they are succeeding.

A Rich Cultural Tapestry

Centuries of invasion, colonization, and trade in Central Asia have produced one of the world's richest and most diverse cultural mixes. Art in Central Asia shows a variety of influences from Greece, Persia, India, and China. The arts were suppressed and controlled during the Soviet era, with artists in traditional art forms such as mosaics forced to depict idealized Communist themes. At the beginning of the twenty-first century, traditional art is reemerging in the five nations, although artistic development is often hampered by a lack of funding.

Early Influences on Central Asian Art

Twenty-five hundred years ago, during the Achaemenid period in Central Asia, the art of the nomads was restricted by the fact that they had no permanent settlements. There are no buildings, monuments, paintings, or sculptures from this period. Yet the nomads showed great creativity in decorating everyday items such as clothing, jewelry, goblets, harnesses, weapons, and caskets. The Scythians, ancient nomads of the steppes in northern Kazakhstan and Siberia, used animal motifs in their decorating that incorporated elements of Assyrian and early Persian art. Bronze objects dating from between 1300 and 1028 B.C. excavated in Ngan-yang, China, were decorated with similar animal motifs, indicating that the stylized animal art of the steppes may have originated in China well before the time of the Scythians.

The animal motifs of the Scythians were replaced by the geometrical and floral motifs of the Samaritans around the third century B.C. The influence of the Scythians and Samaritans spread across the Hunnic tribes of Mongolia, eastern Siberia, and northern China. The art of the Huns incorporated Greek, Assyrian, and Iranian influences as well, and its influence spread across China. According to Edgar

Scythian art, such as this stylized representation of a stag created between 500 and 300 B.C., often depicted animal motifs.

Knobloch, author of *Beyond the Oxus: Archaeology, Art, and Architecture of Central Asia,* "The steppe art influenced Chinese art, and Chinese aesthetics in their turn influenced the art of the nomads."[21]

Greek rule in Central Asia began in the fourth century B.C. and lasted for two centuries. The influence of the Greeks on the arts was very strong, lasting for centuries after their political demise in the area. The integration of Greek and local art can be seen in the depiction of Greek mythical figures combined with ornamental Bactrian motifs. This Graeco-Bactrian art later showed an increased Indian-Buddhist influence and survived in the Kushan period during the first three centuries of the common era. Kushan coins bear images of Greek, Roman, Buddhist, Iranian, and Hindu deities. Kushan art "fused Iranian imperial imagery, Buddhist iconography and Roman realism. . . . Indian, Tibetan and Chinese art were permanently affected."[22]

Sogdian art flourished during the time just before the Arab invasion. The Sogdian style was essentially Persian but also incorporated elements of Zoroastrian, Manichaean, Buddhist, and Christian art with Greek and Indian mythology. Stuccoes, frescoes, and cave temples show examples of these various motifs, which can also be seen in Sogdian jewelry, silverware, and pottery.

The Arab conquest of Central Asia led to a suppression of all traditional art in the region. "Human, animal, and even floral motifs in pottery and metalware, as well as in painting and sculpture, were suppressed and replaced by the only acceptable decoration—the geometrical pattern, the arabesque, combined with the equally geometrical *Kufic* script."[23] Persian influence soon crept back in, however, and Muslim art began to incorporate stylized floral motifs called *islimi*. The rigid *Kufic* script was soon replaced by more flexible and decorative forms of script, and animals and birds—

MANAS

The Kyrgyz national epic *Manas* is a collection of verses that tell of the creation of the Kyrgyz people. The hero of the poems is a strong, brave leader named Manas who struggles to secure the land of his people against invaders from the east. Most modern-day Kyrgyz are familiar with the epic, which celebrated its one-thousandth anniversary in 1995 with a grand festival led by President Askar Akayev. The following verses are from a twentieth-century retelling of the *Manas* epic reprinted in the book *Central Asia* by Bradley Mayhew and his coauthors. They depict the ancient Kyrgyz army as so vast and imposing that onlookers cannot see the towering Altay Mountains, and the earth nearly breaks under their weight.

> Not a space there was between flag and standard;
> the earth's surface could not be seen!
> Not a space there was between banner and standard;
> the range of the Altay could not be seen!
> Points of lances gleamed; men's heads bobbed;
> the earth swayed on the point of collapse.
> Flags on golden standards fluttered,
> and a ground-splitting din was heard . . .
> The army, marching with a terrible noise,
> was greater than the eyes could take in—
> eyes were bowed with all the looking!
> Black plains, grey hills,
> the face of the earth was beaten down!
> Coats of mail all a-glitter,
> racers and chargers bursting forth neighing . . .
> the enormous warrior host
> set a-moving with a crack!

and even the occasional human figure—began to reappear. However, from the eighth century to the present day, art in Central Asia has been predominantly Muslim in nature.

ARCHITECTURE

Virtually no buildings from pre-Islamic times or the first centuries of Arab rule have survived in Central Asia. This is due in part to the destruction wrought by Genghis Khan in the thirteenth century. And in the early twentieth century the Bolsheviks destroyed many religious buildings, sparing only those of architectural or historical value. Most of the monuments to architecture standing in Central Asia today date from the reign of Timur the Lame and his immediate descendants in the fourteenth and fifteenth centuries. Timur brought artists and craftsmen from Persia, Syria, Iraq, the Caucasus, and India to his capital at Samarqand, where they created spectacular examples of architecture, ornament, and decorative art. A typical design element of Timurid architecture is the beautiful, azure-blue dome, which is often ribbed. Cobalt, turquoise, green, and blue tilework with geometric, floral, or calligraphic designs is a hallmark of decoration in Central Asia.

The mosques, or Islamic houses of worship, represent Central Asian architecture at its most striking. Designs vary, but most mosques have arched entrance portals flanked by minarets, which are tall, often tapering towers used to call the faithful to prayer. They are usually circular or conical. The Kalon Minaret in Bukhara is Central Asia's most impressive minaret, at 150 feet high. It was also used as a beacon and watchtower.

The entrance portals of mosques lead to an area containing a series of columns, usually with a roof but sometimes open, and a covered area for prayer. The entrance to some mosques, such as the Bolo-hauz in Bukhara, has a flat, brightly painted roof supported by columns. Other mosques, such as the Juma Mosque in Khiva, consist of an enclosed court with a roof resting on rows of beautifully carved wooden columns. The focal point of all mosques is the *mihrab*, a niche that faces the direction of Mecca.

Muslim architecture is also seen in *madrasahs*, which are Islamic colleges. They usually consist of an inner courtyard surrounded by one- or two-story buildings that include a

This university, built during the fifteenth to seventeenth century, features an azure-blue dome (right), a typical Timurid architectural element.

mosque, lecture rooms, living quarters for students and teachers, and prayer cells. In the middle of each of the four courtyard walls is usually a decorated *iwan*, an arched portal. The Registran in Samarqand contains a majestic ensemble of *madrasahs*, including the Sher Dor, which has two large panels that flaunt Islamic tradition by depicting a striped tiger attacking a deer beneath a Mongol-faced sun.

Another type of Muslim architecture in Central Asia is the mausoleum, a large and elaborate tomb, usually built by a ruler for himself or his family. Most mausoleums consist of a domed structure above a prayer room, with the actual grave housed in a central hall or an underground room. One of the most famous mausoleums in Central Asia is the tomb of the Mongol ruler Timur in Samarqand, the Gur Emir. *Beyond the Oxus* contains the following description of the mausoleum, which was built in 1404:

> [Gur Emir] is still a monumental and dramatic structure. Externally it is divided into three equal parts. A bulbous dome, 112 feet high, is enriched with 64 almost round flutes and flanked by minarets 83 feet high. It is

set on a high but narrower cylindrical drum which causes a sharp constriction at the base of the dome. This drum, in turn, rises out of a chamber which, on the exterior, is octagonal. Portals pierce each of the major four sides, again reminiscent of ancient Sasanian practice. The dome is covered with bright blue tiles and the high drum, ornamented with a huge inscription of rectangular Kufic, is of golden-buff bricks. The interior is also impressive, with an alabaster dado [lower section of the wall], grey-green jasper cornice [top section of the wall], black limestone niches and a marble balustrade [railing].[24]

The Ismail Samani Mausoleum in Bukhara was completed around 905. It has baked terra-cotta brickwork and is decorated with Zoroastrian symbols such as the circle in nested squares. The huge, double-domed Sultan Sanjar Mausoleum in Merv was built in the twelfth century. A blue-and-red frieze that adorns the upper gallery is being restored. These two mausoleums are among the only structures to have survived the destruction during the reign of Genghis Khan. This is probably due to their thick walls—the Ismail Samani's walls are six feet thick, and the Sultan Sanjar's are almost ten feet thick.

Secular architecture in Central Asia includes palaces and covered bazaars. The Tosh Khovli Palace was built between 1832 and 1841. It has 150 rooms off nine courtyards and is decorated with geometric-motif ceramic tiles and carved stone and wood. The brightly patterned high ceilings are held up by carved wooden pillars. Several sixteenth-century domed bazaars have survived in Bukhara. These were usually built over intersections of busy streets—two or more streets run beneath them. These structures were built for practical purposes and are not decorated, but they have a unique architectural character. A main cupola (dome roof) stands over the actual crossroads, and around it are several smaller and lower cupolas covering the shops.

FOLK ART

While the architecture of Central Asia is often striking and artistically sophisticated, throughout history the people of Central Asia have also produced smaller works of art that serve a functional purpose. Carved screens and doors, brightly colored carpets, woven mats, and leather bottles used for carrying *kumys* (fermented mare's milk) are still produced and sold in bazaars in the streets of cities such as Bukhara and Ashkhabad. Plant and animal designs have been popular motifs throughout the centuries. The region has also traditionally emphasized equestrian culture, and horses are an especially popular design for works of art such as decorative blankets, saddles, and head and neck ornaments. Because Islam prohibits the depiction of human or animal forms, Muslim art, especially that used to decorate mosques, emphasizes calligraphy (the artistic rendering of Arabic script), arabesque (floral and geometric designs, sometimes with embedded calligraphy), and elaborate prayer rugs.

Workers restore the intricate terra-cotta brickwork on the Ismail Samani Mausoleum in Bukhara.

Other works of traditional and functional art are still produced and highly valued in Central Asia. The *tus-kiiz*, or "wall carpet," was traditionally used to cover bedding or decorate the walls of yurts. A *tus-kiiz* is usually made of red or brightly colored velvet, with embroidered silk panels bordering the top and bottom. Plant, flower, bird, and other animal designs are featured.

Heavy felt rugs called *shyrdaks* are made by hand in Kyrgyzstan. These consist of multiple layers of pounded felt in varying colors, with the upper layers cut in a pattern to reveal the colors of the layers beneath. Uzbek coverlets made of silk and cotton, called *suzani*, employ floral or celestial motifs. These are used as table covers, wall hangings, cushions, or bedspreads.

Traditional and functional art such as carpets, carved doors, and pottery is highly valued in Central Asia.

Tashkent's Museum of Applied Arts has examples of *suzani*, textiles, and embossed metal arts. Central Asian jewelry tends to be elaborate with intricate designs. A combination of silver and precious stones such as lapis lazuli and

carnelian is popular. Stone molds used for casting earrings dating back to the first century B.C. have been found in Uzbekistan. These two-thousand-year-old earrings look as modern as any available today.

LITERATURE

While some artists were producing carpets and jewelry, others were producing epic literature. Because literacy in Central Asia was not widespread until the twentieth century, the region's literature began in oral form. Songs, poems, and stories were made popular by traveling storytellers who sang or recited them to crowds. Some of these traveling storytellers, called *akyn*, became folk heroes. In fact, *akyn* competitions are still held in some rural areas today.

The Kyrgyz oral epic *Manas* is a poem of several hundred thousand lines and many different versions that deals with the hero Manas's struggle against invaders to his land. Like the Uzbek epic *Alpamish, Manas* dates back one thousand years. The Turkmen also continue to value their oral literary tradition, which includes the epic tales *Korkut Ata* and *Gurogly*. Kazakhstan's oral histories include the sixteenth-century *Koblandy-batir, Er Sain*, and *Er Targyn*. These were often chanted to the accompaniment of drums and the *dombra*, a string instrument.

Literature also took written form. A tenth-century Sāmānid court poet named Abū 'Abdollāh Rūdaki is considered the "father of Persian literature." The poet Omar Khayyám, who spent part of his early life in Samarqand, is the author of the famous collection of quatrains known as *The Rubáiyát of Omar Khayyám*. The "father of Turkmen literature," the poet Magtumguly Feraghy, is regarded by the people of Turkmenistan almost as a saint—his words are said to be as revered as those of the Qur'an. A nineteenth-century Kazakh writer named Abay Kunabaev translated Russian and other foreign literature into Kazakh, and his own works helped launch Kazakh as a literary language. The twentieth-century writer Mirzo Tursunzoda collected Tajik oral literature and wrote poetry about social change in Tajikistan.

The modern writer Chinghis Aitmatov of Kyrgyzstan became one of the best-known artists of the Soviet era. He is the only Central Asian writer to gain international acclaim. His works have been published in Kyrgyz and Russian; translated

SETORA: THE "TASHKENT SPICE GIRLS"

The latest music video by Setora, a trio of young Uzbek women dubbed the "Tashkent Spice Girls," shows unmistakable overtones of military propaganda. Setora appears in the video wearing tight khaki clothes and singing and dancing with Uzbek soldiers. In the video, one of the girls is in love with a soldier who is on a mission to rescue a mother and her three children from a kidnapper, who is a stereotypical political enemy of Uzbekistan. In an article titled "Military Music Videos as Uzbek Pop Propaganda" (available at www.cacianalyst.org), writer Chris Aslan says,

> The kidnapper is a fat, bearded, leering Islamic fundamentalist, wearing a Palestinian headdress, just in case anyone has failed to make the connection. When discovered, the fundamentalist clutches a vulnerable small child with a knife to his throat. Our hero then dives to the rescue, saves the little boy's life but is gunned down in the process. The video jumps to the three grieving, and still singing "Tashkent Spice Girls" mournfully droop[ing] over the heroic soldier's coffin at the military funeral, while the little boy is shown in slow motion romping free and happy in the park.

into English, German, and French, and adapted for the stage and screen in the former USSR and abroad.

MUSIC

The development of Central Asian music was closely tied to their literary tradition, because many poems and epic stories were sung to the accompaniment of musical instruments. Traditional Central Asian music has Middle Eastern and Persian influences. The musical instruments used are similar to Arabic instruments. Stringed instruments include the *rabab*, a six-stringed mandolin; the *dutar*, a two-stringed lute; the *dombra*, a two-stringed Kazakh guitar; the *kobyz*, a two-stringed primitive fiddle; and the *zhetigen*, a stringed instrument with a rectangular body and seven strings. Percussion instruments include the *dabyl* and *dauylpaz*, small, hand-held drums, and the *doira*, a tambourine or drum. A Central Asian wind instrument, the *sybyzgy*, is made of two reed or wood flutes strapped together.

Sozanda is a popular form of folk music in Uzbek and Tajik societies. *Sozanda* is accompanied only by percussion instruments and is sung primarily by women. The folk music of Turkmenistan combines influences from Persia, Azerbaijan, and Turkey. It features drums, accordions, and lutes.

Central Asia is also home to modern pop music, such as that of the successful Uzbek group Yalla. The music of Yalla features a mixture of Central Asian and Middle Eastern folk melodies with modern pop influences. Another group, Setora, is a successful trio whose music videos are popular on Uzbek television.

MOVIES

Central Asian musicians have also found work composing and performing the scores for movies. The region had a long history of producing films for the Soviet Union during the twentieth century. After independence there was a drop in the number of films produced, but in the late 1990s that trend began to change. In 1998, the first Eurasia Film Festival was held in Almaty, the former capital of Kazakhstan. And

Traditional Central Asian instruments include the oboelike surnai *(left) and large horns called* karnai *(far right).*

Besh Kumpyr (Five Old Ladies), a Kyrgyz film, was a finalist in the Grand Prix in Cannes, France.

Kazakhstan is by far the largest film producer in Central Asia. Recent releases include *Lost Love of Genghis Khan; Shankhai*, a movie about urban life; and *Abay*, a movie about the Kazakh literary hero Abay Kunabaev. The 1999 Karlovy Vary Film Festival in the Czech Republic brought international attention to Kazakh films, which tend to be heavily influenced by their tradition of nomadic existence on the steppes. Yermek Shinarbayev, one of Kazakhstan's leading film directors who often portrays nomadic themes in his films, says, "There is a sense on the steppe that you can go anywhere. You can see the horizon and move off in any direction you choose."[25]

Like so many other areas of life in Central Asia, the arts have been deemphasized in recent years as the new nations have had to cope with a complete restructuring of their economic and political systems. But the long history of the Central Asians' achievement in architecture, textiles, metalwork, literature, and music indicates that a new era of creativity will likely begin in the near future.

CONFLICT AND COOPERATION ALONG THE NEW SILK ROAD

With vast natural resources, a literate and resourceful populace, and enthusiasm stemming from recent independence, the Central Asian States are ripe for rapid economic development and political reform. Yet there are many obstacles to progress: ethnic conflicts, poor transportation and utility systems, lack of capital, entrenched bureaucracies, and political repression. These economic and political factors in the region are shaping life today, leaving both the region's inhabitants and outside observers wondering if the promise of democracy and prosperity will be fulfilled.

REGIONAL DIPLOMACY

As in past centuries, powerful nations have vied with one another for influence and control in Central Asia. In many ways Russia is still the most important influence that the Central Asian States must deal with, but the newly independent states have other suitors as well—and some Central Asian leaders are not above letting them compete for influence. In the coming decades, regional powers such as China, Turkey, Iran, and India will be important factors in the development of Central Asia, and Western Europe and the United States will likely also have increasing influence. The task for Central Asian leaders is to manage these competing interests in such a way that they lead to real progress—without igniting the sort of intense and even violent rivalries that have been seen in the past.

For example, China has a problem in its western autonomous province of Xinjiang: A sizable portion of the population belongs to the Uyghur ethnic group, who are Muslim. The Chinese have suppressed Islam in the province, and some Uyghurs have formed guerrilla groups to battle government troops. Though Muslims in neighboring Kazakhstan, Kyrgyzstan, and Tajikistan are sympathetic to the guerrillas' cause, China wants the Central Asian States to deny sanctuary to the militants. In general, the new Central Asian nations have seen this as being in their best interests. The Dushanbe Declaration, which came out of a meeting in 2000 between leaders of China and the Central Asian States, says that the countries agree to work together to stop "separatism, terrorism, and extremism" from affecting Central Asia. Although those goals sound noble, the declaration may be used to justify further restrictions on religious practice and freedom of speech, both by China and by the Central Asian States.

POLITICAL REPRESSION INCREASES

The end of Communist rule in Central Asia has not always meant freedom from political repression and human rights violations. Writing in June 2000, Rachel Denber of Human Rights Watch said that "almost all of the [Central Asian States] have in fact already completed their transition away from communism. However, the transitions have been not fully to democracy but to various forms of authoritarianism that will jeopardize human rights protections in the foreseeable future."[26] For example, Uzbekistan and Turkmenistan have eliminated political parties opposed to the government, and opposition leaders have been either jailed or forced to leave the country. Tajikistan has used force to put down opposition in its northern region, and the government of Kazakhstan has used a variety of tactics to ensure its continuation in power, including manipulating the media and elections. And in Kyrgyzstan, which shortly after independence instituted important democratic reforms, opposition leader Felix Kulov was arrested in March 2000 on what the International League for Human Rights and others believe were trumped-up charges. He was acquitted and released from jail in August, but his arrest and trial were chilling reminders that the Central Asian States have a long way to go before achieving the freedoms that people in the West take for granted.

One very modern freedom in the West is access to the Internet. The ability to communicate freely about political and

MANY LANGUAGES, MANY ALPHABETS

An issue that is much on the minds of people in Central Asia these days is one that people in most other parts of the world take for granted—their alphabet. That the alphabet is an issue at all is an indication of the degree to which the region has been subject to conquest and colonization over the centuries.

Most of the languages of the native societies of the region derive from Turkic, which is the origin of modern Turkish as well as Kazakh, Kyrgyz, Turkmen, and Uzbek. Tajik is derived from Persian. All these languages can be written in the Arabic alphabet, and this is fairly common in Tajikistan, which has (by a slight margin) the highest proportion of Muslims—90 percent—and which tends to be the most conservative. However, because of 150 years of Russian and Soviet colonization and control of the region, the most common alphabet in use today is Cyrillic, the alphabet in which Russian is written.

But the newly independent states want to rid themselves of the vestiges of the colonial period and become part of the modern world, in which the Latin alphabet is dominant. The governments of Central Asia have announced plans to switch to the Latin alphabet or variants of it. For example, in 1995 Uzbekistan announced that its official alphabet would be standard Latin minus the letters *c* and *w*, whose sounds are not used in Uzbek, and assigning other sounds used in Uzbek to combinations of letters and the apostrophe, for example, *o', g', sh, ch,* and *ng.*

Another aspect of this is the use of diacritical marks, which are the marks that indicate a shift in sound. Diacritical marks are not used for English words except when they are derived from other languages, especially French. For example, the word *fiancé* uses the acute accent to indicate that the final *e* is pronounced like a long *a.* Diacriticals were once an efficient way to convey meaning and sound, but they have run into a peculiarly modern problem. The problem is that computer keyboards have been developed for unaccented English. Even though computers can produce all diacriticals, they require more keystrokes and thus slow down and complicate the process of typing. This is why, in the coming decades, the languages of Central Asia will likely be written in an unaccented Latin alphabet.

social issues that the Internet has brought to much of the world is seen as a threat by the governments of Central Asia. As reporter Bea Hogan says, "Information is power, and nowhere is this axiom clearer than in former communist Central Asian countries, where governments' power rests on keeping their citizens isolated and ill informed."[27] For example, in early 2000 Kazakhstan required all Internet traffic to be routed through a central government office that can monitor communications. The agency responsible for the system has established classifications for Internet users, one of which allows the government to view all of the person's Internet activities as they are happening, to decode or destroy e-mail messages, to stop an Internet connection, and even to disconnect service entirely. This has been done even though Kazakh law guarantees the right to send and receive information and the right to privacy for all forms of communication.

In Turkmenistan, the government instituted licensing restrictions that have shut down all the Internet service providers except one, Turkmen Telecom, which is run by the government. Even though the government did not institute the sort of strict monitoring used in Kazakhstan, the fact that it now controls all Internet traffic in the country will allow it to stifle the political opposition, as it did by shutting down their websites prior to the 1999 parliamentary elections.

ECONOMIC PROBLEMS AND OPPORTUNITIES

The nations of Central Asia have the potential to be prosperous members of the global economy. They have valuable natural resources in the form of fertile agricultural areas; deposits of minerals, oil, and gas; and a well-educated populace. Since independence, however, in many ways the countries have become poorer: Crop yields are down, unemployment is up, and the oil and gas fields are undeveloped because of disagreements over the pipelines necessary to get the products to market.

One problem area has been the agriculture industry in Uzbekistan, which is heavily dependent on cotton. Because cotton is the major crop grown in the country, unfavorable weather or a disease that decreases the cotton crop spells disaster for the Uzbek economy. For example, cool, wet weather in 1992 lowered the cotton yield significantly and put many Uzbeks out of work. Efforts to increase the planting of other crops have been only partly successful because the country's farmers are only familiar with the techniques of growing cotton, and their machinery is not designed to handle food crops. Diversifying Uzbekistan's agriculture will be a long-term project, perhaps taking decades to complete.

In Kazakhstan, President Nursultan Nazarbayev has instituted market reforms and attracted Western investment, particularly for the development of the country's oil and gas reserves, but getting them out of the ground and to market is a difficult problem. In Turkmenistan, President Saparmurat Niyazov also promises to develop his country's oil and gas reserves, but his highly personal and autocratic style of governing has probably impeded foreign investment. Several pipeline plans are being considered, but pipelines require a huge capital investment, large and sustained production volume, and international cooperation, in this case involving Turkey, Azerbaijan, Georgia, Kazakhstan, and Turkmenistan, as well as the United States, Russia, and Iran, and multinational oil corporations like BP-Amoco.

Politicians in Central Asia are acutely aware of the economic problems facing their countries, and their public statements sound very much like those of politicians in the

Workers load cotton onto a truck in Uzbekistan, a country that is economically dependent on the crop.

THE FATE OF THE BAYKONUR COSMODROME

The Baykonur Cosmodrome, one of the world's largest space-ports, was a Soviet missile- and rocket-testing facility from which satellites and interplanetary probes were launched. In 1961 it was the launch site of Yury Gagarin, the first man to orbit the earth. The cosmodrome is 186 miles southwest of the town of Baykonur, in Kazakhstan. The nearest town is Leninsk, which was built to guard and service the cosmodrome.

After the collapse of the USSR, the fate of the Baykonur Cosmodrome was in question. Russia wanted the cosmodrome to itself, but Kazakhstan wanted joint ownership. As Russia and Kazakhstan debated ownership of the cosmodrome during the early 1990s, the facility deteriorated due to the region's harsh climate and to theft by employees. Because of a lack of funds, there was a suspension of many space projects during this time, and a corresponding fall in living standards in nearby towns. Finally, in 1994, Kazakhstan agreed to lease the Baykonur Cosmodrome and the nearby town of Leninsk to Russia for twenty years, at a cost of $120 million per year.

Russia continues to launch satellites from Baykonur, including the *Zvezda* service module, which lifted off on July 12, 2000. The *Zvezda* linked up with the International Space Station in order to provide electricity, propulsion, and living quarters for the sixteen-nation space outpost. However, there is a federal program under consideration in Russia that would gradually shift spacecraft launchings from Baykonur to the Plesetsk Cosmodrome in the Arkhangel'sk region. The aim of this program is to guarantee Russia access to outer space from its own territory.

Russia launched the Zvezda *service module from the Baykonur Cosmodrome in Kazakhstan in 2000.*

West. For example, President Askar Akayev of Kyrgyzstan has said, "Currently, the most important goals facing society as a whole are to intensify positive trends in the economy and make them stable, to encourage and support national entrepreneurship, especially on the part of small and medium-sized businesses, to attract direct investment and to make extensive use of new technology."[28] The difficulty in Kyrgyzstan and the other Central Asian States was that, at least at the beginning of the twenty-first century, their main value to the outside world was in their natural resources and agriculture and not in their technological sophistication. Companies from the Americas, Europe, and East Asia saw little reason to invest in the new nations for two reasons. First, the labor pool, although literate, did not have large numbers of technicians on the leading edge of their fields. And second, political repression and instability make companies hesitate to put substantial sums into buildings, equipment, and training. So while President Akayev called for high-tech investment in Kyrgyzstan, his own policies of suppressing political dissent made it unlikely that major international companies would risk investing there.

CONFLICTS

The economic problems of the Central Asian States set the stage for a variety of conflicts. Water, especially for agriculture, is a major bone of contention among the Central Asian States for several reasons. First, the geographic area known as the Aral Sea Basin is the principal watershed for all five countries of Central Asia, but decisions about water can be made by each country individually, and the countries do not always agree on the best use of the water. Second, the Aral Sea itself was devastated by a Soviet policy of diverting water for agriculture from the rivers that flow into it. Beginning in the 1960s and continuing almost unchanged since independence, this has caused the Aral to shrink to half its pre-1960 size. In itself, the shrinking of the lake is an environmental disaster for the area's wildlife and the populations that depend directly on the lake, but its drying up has also had worldwide consequences. The salt and dust left behind have contributed to huge toxic sandstorms that have damaged crops, buildings, and the health of livestock and people hundreds of miles away. They have also increased the

A man stands on the fishing boat he used to skipper before the drying of the Aral Sea.

amount of dust in the air worldwide, which may have climate and other consequences that are difficult to predict.

The problem is not that there is too little water but, rather, that too much of the water available is wasted. The region is still dependent on cotton as the main cash crop, and cotton requires huge amounts of water to grow, especially using the inefficient distribution and irrigation systems of the region. This problem may take decades to be solved, if it ever is, because the countries are poor. They have few resources to make the needed changes and often concentrate on short-term goals, such as ensuring the health of the next cotton crop, rather than long-term goals, such as building better irrigation systems, switching to less water-intensive crops, and restoring the health of the Aral Sea.

Now that decisions about water use are more in the hands of the region's governments, they may realize that they will have to live with the environmental consequences of their decisions. The countries have signed three water-management agreements since independence and now have commissions with representatives from all the countries for both the Amu and Syr Rivers, which cross the region and flow into the Aral Sea.

Still, conflicts arise as countries attempt to define and pursue their interests. In 1997, Uzbekistan briefly reduced the flow of the Syr River into Kazakhstan, threatening the Kazakh cotton crop. The flow was restored only after riots by Kazakh farmers. And after a meeting on water policy in March 2000, President Niyazov of Turkmenistan said that countries should first try to solve their water problems internally and then work out deals with their immediate neighbors, a policy that seems to contradict both rhetoric and treaties on international cooperation.

In the summer of 2000, a severe drought reduced crop yields in the region. Tajikistan was hardest hit, and its problems highlight the dangers facing all the Central Asian States. First, even though growing conditions were good as recently as 1997, Tajikistan was not able to store grain or convert it to cash because even in good years it has to import grain, needing hundreds of thousands of tons to feed its people. Second, farming methods are becoming increasingly primitive as farm machinery from the Soviet era wears out and there is no money to either fix or replace the equipment. Thus, many tasks once done by tractors, trucks, and harvesters are now done by hand. Finally, the irrigation system is also suffering from lack of maintenance. The amount of land under irrigation has dropped drastically as parts of the system have had to be shut down. These factors make Tajikistan more vulnerable to droughts, and to varying degrees these problems are shared by all the countries of Central Asia. The result is that international aid organizations like the United Nations are asked to provide assistance. But the extent of the drought-related food shortages may be so great that many people in the region will experience malnutrition in the coming decades.

ENVIRONMENTAL CONCERNS

The health of the environment in Central Asia is a major issue, though at times it seems more of a concern to other nations than it does to the Central Asian States themselves—especially to their governments. This is understandable. The newly independent nations inherited major problems that resulted from environmental policy being decided by a distant government during the Soviet era, a need for huge investment in new systems and equipment to remedy past mistakes, and current economic woes. The governments, as in so many areas, seem forced to concentrate on survival and either ignore or gloss over environmental problems.

The Soviets were interested in Central Asia mainly as a producer of cotton, and their policies were directed to that end, with apparently little thought for the environmental consequences. Russia had great success in increasing Central Asian cotton production in the 1960s and '70s. But by the late 1980s production had fallen 20 percent because the soil was becoming less fertile and residues of pesticides and herbicides used to boost yields were reaching such high levels that they were damaging crops, workers, and even those living in the area who had nothing to do with cotton farming. The Soviet overemphasis on cotton production to the exclusion of all other crops made the regional economy unstable because it depended so heavily on the success of the cotton crop each year—and no agricultural crop is that reliable. Drought, flood, insects, and disease can all destroy a year's crop, and the Central Asian States had few sources of income other than cotton to fall back on. In their desperation to maintain cotton production, the nations have often seen it as an unfortunate necessity to sacrifice environmental concerns for the sake of cash flow.

Alternatives to cotton that the Central Asian States are currently developing are their oil, gas, and mineral resources, but of course these also carry substantial environmental risks. For example, in the summer of 2000, a Kazakh oil company operating off the country's Caspian Sea coast was suspected of contributing to the death of nearly ten thousand seals when oil wastes were found in their bodies. The company denied the accusation, but large-scale oil production has been associated with many environmental problems. Because of their eagerness to generate revenue, both oil company employees and government officials face close scrutiny from critics who fear that good environmental practice may take second place to rapid exploration and production.

A Kazakh resident burns the bodies of dead seals, which were poisoned by oil wastes suspected to have come from an oil company operating off the country's Caspian Sea coast.

In Kyrgyzstan, the Kumtor Gold Company, which was formed in 1996 by the Kyrgyz government and a Canadian mining company, has been mining a gold deposit. According to Maria Utyaganova of the American University in Kyrgyzstan, the country "attracts a lot of foreign mining and metallurgic companies to a large extent by its soft environmental laws. The Kyrgyz government invites foreign companies because they are very profitable for Kyrgyzstan's developing economy."[29] Aside from direct damage to the land from mining, the primary hazard in gold mining comes from the use of cyanide, a poison, to remove the gold from the ore. In 1998, a truck containing two tons of cyanide drove into a river that flowed into Lake Issyk-Kul, the largest lake in Kyrgyzstan. The disaster, however, prompted Kumtor to increase environmental safety measures, and in 1999 the mine reported no major pollution incidents.

In May 2000 in the northern Kazakh town of Petropavlovsk, a leak in a storage facility sent three tons of diesel fuel into the Ishim River, the source of drinking water for much of the region's population. Three days later a huge fire broke out along the river where the fuel had soaked into the ground and foliage. According to reporter Marat Yermukanov of the Petropavlovsk *Tribuna*, accidents like this highlight many of the ecological problems in Central Asia. The fuel leak and fire happened during a local environmental cleanup campaign and despite the fact that the city is home to an internationally funded environmental project, the Petropavlovsk Ecocenter. Yermukanov cites public apathy as the major problem, saying that people are not accustomed to even hearing about environmental problems, much less being encouraged to take an active role in solving them. And he says that the ecocenter, though its monitoring and education projects are worthwhile, is not able to mobilize the public to take effective action.

AFGHANISTAN, ISLAM, AND DRUGS

Just as Central Asia's environmental woes have consequences for neighboring countries, the political problems of neighboring countries have consequences for the Central Asian States. For example, Afghanistan, which shares a border with Tajikistan, Uzbekistan, and Turkmenistan, has been the site of many wars waged by both the armies of other countries and native factions for the last two hundred years. Since 1973 the country has endured almost continuous fighting. In 1996, a militia called the Taliban, which means "religious students," captured the capital, Kabul, and began to establish what they call the purest Islamic state in the world (though many Muslim leaders think the Taliban's version of Islam is misguided). The Taliban are a problem for the Central Asian States for two reasons. First, they fund their activities in Afghanistan largely with the proceeds from drug dealing—Afghanistan produces as much as 75 percent of the world opium supply. Second, the

FREEDOM OF THE PRESS IN KYRGYZSTAN

Though the constitution of Kyrgyzstan guarantees freedom of the press, during the 1990s and especially as the country's presidential election approached in October 2000, there were many signs that the government was doing everything it could to limit the press's ability to report on political issues. The leading independent newspaper in Kyrgyzstan, *Res Publica*, was fined an amount equal to its entire annual budget for publishing an unfavorable story about a public official, and the paper's editor, Zamira Sydykova, was jailed, sent to a labor camp, and twice banned from journalism for eighteen months. Nevertheless, Sydykova found ways to continue publishing *Res Publica*, and she attracted important help from outside Central Asia: The AOL–Time Warner company agreed to help fund *Res Publica*, and Sydykova was given the 2000 "Courage in Journalism Award" from the International Women's Media Foundation. In an interview with *Eurasia Insight* following the announcement of the award ("Press Freedom Suffers during Kyrgyzstan's Presidential Campaign," available at www.Eurasianet.org), Sydykova said,

> We're experiencing a lot of different pressures. . . . The government . . . has stepped up the repression that is going on in the country, especially in respect to independent media. . . . We are experiencing financial pressures. . . . The situation is affecting all independent-minded publication in the country. . . . A lot of people in our country—who are really great at what they do, who by rights should really be the politicians in power—they have been excluded from the presidential elections. And this was done under various circumstances. For example, they are entangled in different trials going on in the republic. And so they do not have the necessary means to enter a presidential election. And they have also been excluded for not knowing the Kyrgyz language that well. . . . And thus many good and honorable people did not have the opportunity to take part in this process. . . . During the parliamentary elections, the authorities figured out all the possible violations and fraud they could get away with. . . . Political parties and journalists are protesting, but nothing is really happening as a result. So they see that they can continue to engage in fraud and do whatever they feel is necessary to win the election. . . . Journalists are being harassed. . . . And everything is being done so that freedom-minded publications will not reach their readers.

Taliban want other Muslim countries in the region to have Islamic revolutions similar to theirs in Afghanistan. The Taliban seem to be involved in guerrilla insurgencies in Tajikistan and Uzbekistan, which border Afghanistan; in fact, problems stemming from activities sponsored or supported by the Taliban reach as far north as Kyrgyzstan. According to Kyrgyz economist Kunduz Sydygaliova,

> The unstable situations in Tajikistan and Afghanistan have allowed narcotics traffickers to transport opium through the Gornyi-Badakhshan [Tajikistan] region to southern Kyrgyzstan. This route has turned into a transit corridor for narcotics to Central Asia . . . Europe, and the U.S. The northern Chui region of Kyrgyzstan has already become a key distributive point for international narcotics smugglers. Narcotics trafficking is one of the main sources of financing for international terrorism and religious extremism in the region. Traffickers thrive on political and social instability to support their activities. They know that a lasting peace in Central Asia, including Afghanistan, would negatively impact their illicit business.[30]

To deal with the threat of armed insurgencies by Islamic militants, Uzbekistan announced in the summer of 2000 that it would restructure its military to be more "mobile, self-sufficient and flexible."[31] Uzbek troops had skirmishes with insurgents on several occasions and reported that the guerrillas were well armed with sophisticated weapons. The Uzbeks got commitments of help from Russia, which promised to supply border surveillance equipment and surface-to-air missiles, which can be used both to target the planes of the drug traffickers who help to fund the insurgents and to discourage air attacks by neighboring countries. In the spring of 2000, U.S. secretary of state Madeline Albright visited Tashkent, Uzbekistan, and promised $10 million to train and equip security forces and provide military all-terrain vehicles for the Fergana Valley.

RUSSIAN INFLUENCES

Russia, both before and during the Soviet era, has been the most important foreign influence in Central Asia. Since independence, Russian strength in the region has varied be-

U.S. secretary of state Madeline Albright (in hat) visited Tashkent, Uzbekistan, in 2000, promising U.S. funds to help resist attacks by neighboring countries.

cause the newly independent states have wanted to assert their autonomy and at the same time to avoid angering their large and powerful neighbor to the north, on whom they depend heavily for economic and military assistance.

Vladimir Putin, who became president of Russia in 2000, soon began looking for ways to again increase Russia's role in Central Asia, promising increased military and economic aid if the new nations will support Russia in international forums like the United Nations and in negotiations over oil and gas pipelines, which Russia wants to pass through Russian territory. Putin's most visible form of aid was an estimated twenty-five thousand troops in southern Tajikistan who patrolled the

border with Afghanistan in an effort to reduce drug trafficking and terrorist attacks. The Moscow government also
planned to establish a military base in Tajikistan to facilitate
training and coordination, and according to reporter Joseph
Fritchett, discussions were under way to provide some air defense capability to Tajikistan. (At the time, Uzbekistan had the
only air force in the region.) Fritchett writes, "This Russian
success in establishing a permanent military presence in
Tajikistan amounts to a geopolitical breakthrough for Mr.
Putin. It is the first such accord in the region since the countries gained their independence after the Cold War."[32]

RELATIONS WITH THE UNITED STATES

The United States has generally tried to avoid becoming too
involved in the affairs of the Central Asian States. According
to foreign policy analysts, Central Asia is too far away and its
problems too complex for the United States to be effective
in the region. On the other hand, the United States has offered military assistance in the one area in which it has a
clear interest, the war on illegal drugs, and it wants to play a
part in decisions about the routes for oil and gas pipelines
in the region. This may put the United States at odds with
Central Asian governments, which propose pipeline routes
that go through Central Asia and Iran; the United States fa-
vors routes that pass through Turkey, an ally, and not
through Iran, which has been in conflict with the United
States ever since U.S. diplomats were held hostage in Iran
from 1979 to 1981. Reporter Joseph Fritchett visited Central
Asia in the summer of 2000 and interviewed U.S. officials sta-
tioned there. According to Fritchett,

> "Pipelines are not a zero-sum game," a U.S. official said,
> referring to the Clinton administration's efforts to get
> the investment, transit fees and other benefits of
> Caspian Sea pipelines to Turkey, a Western ally. This ap-
> proach has involved trying to keep pipelines, with their
> earnings and political leverage, away from Iran and,
> where possible, Russia, even though routes across both
> countries made economic sense. Instead, plans have
> been delayed, and Central Asian governments blame
> their economic woes partly on U.S. preoccupation with
> punishing Iran.[33]

One indication of the U.S. government's view of the situation in Central Asia was the funding plan the U.S. Agency for International Development (USAID) released in September 2000. The agency funds a wide variety of programs aimed at increasing democracy and economic opportunity around the world, but it makes its plans based on what it sees as actually possible in each country. In Central Asia, it seemed that US-AID felt that the chances for extensive reform and progress were slim because the agency proposed maintaining existing levels of aid in Kazakhstan and Kyrgyzstan and reducing aid to Tajikistan, Turkmenistan, and Uzbekistan. According to human rights expert Erika Dailey, the approach taken by US-AID probably means that the United States is waiting for autocratic leaders like Uzbekistan's Islam Karimov and Turkmenistan's Saparmurat Niyazov to leave office before attempting major democracy-building programs. According to Dailey, "The disappointment implicit in the report is well-founded. Civil and political freedoms are protected unreliably (Kazakhstan and Kyrgyzstan), are virtually absent (Tajikistan and Uzbekistan), or are entirely absent (Turkmenistan). Despite eight years of international development assistance, civil society is in a profound crisis in Central Asia."[34]

THE NEW NATIONS IN THE NEW CENTURY

The modest efforts of the United States to influence Central Asia seem to be based on the realization that the newly independent nations cannot be controlled by it or any foreign power. Central Asia has been disputed territory politically and economically for over twenty-five hundred years. In the new century, the Central Asian States' neighbors, especially Russia, China, Afghanistan, and Iran, as well as nations around the world, will continue to vie for roles in the region. But despite similarities to the conflicts of past centuries, the first decade of independence demonstrated that the Central Asian States have made a new start. Independence has given them recognition and the protection of international law, making it unlikely that they will again have to endure military conquest. Though their first efforts at building democratic institutions and economic prosperity have often been deeply flawed, it is clear that the fate of the region is more than ever in the hands of its own people and leaders.

FACTS ABOUT THE CENTRAL ASIAN STATES

KAZAKHSTAN

Geography

Area: 1,049,141 square miles

Topography: More than three-fourths of the country is desert or semi-desert, with elevations below sea level along the Caspian Sea coast. The Altay Shan and Tian Shan mountain ranges cover about 12 percent of the country and reach elevations of nearly 23,000 feet.

Rivers: Syr Dar'ya and Irtysh

Climate: Dry except in the eastern mountains, where snowfall is heavy; wide seasonal temperature variation.

Government

Capital: Astana

Date of independence: December 16, 1991

Government type: Republic

President: Nursultan Nazarbayev

People

Population: 16,846,808 (1998)

Ethnic groups: Kazakh, 41.9 percent; Russian, 46 percent; Ukrainian, 4.9 percent; German, 3.1 percent

Official languages: Kazakh, Russian

Religions: Sunni Muslim, 47 percent; Russian Orthodox, 44 percent; Protestant, 2 percent

Economy

Monetary unit: tenge

Exchange rate: 148.4 = US $1 (Oct. 1999)

Labor force: Industry, 27 percent; agriculture and forestry, 23 percent

Gross domestic product per capita: $3,000

KYRGYZSTAN

Geography

Area: 76,641 square miles

Topography: Tian Shan, Pamir, and Alai mountain ranges dominate the area, with an average elevation of 9,022 feet. The mountains contain deep valleys and glaciers; many lakes and fast-flowing rivers drain from the mountains. There are flat expanses in the northern and eastern valleys.

Rivers: Naryn and Chatkal

Climate: Continental with wide variation between mountain valleys and flatlands; precipitation is high in the western mountains and low in the north-central region.

Government

Capital: Bishkek

Date of independence: November 20, 1990

Government type: Republic

President: Askar Akayev

People

Population: 4,522,281 (1998)

Ethnic groups: Kyrgyz, 52.4 percent; Russian, 18 percent; Uzbek, 12.9 percent; Ukrainian, 2.5 percent; German, 2.4 percent; other, 11.8 percent

Official languages: Kyrgyz, Russian

Religions: Sunni Muslim, 75 percent; Russian Orthodox, 20 percent

Economy

Monetary unit: som

Exchange rate: 40.75 = US $1 (Oct. 1999)

Labor force: Agriculture and forestry, 40 percent; industry and construction, 19 percent

Gross domestic product per capita: $2,100

TAJIKISTAN

Geography

Area: 55,251 square miles

Topography: Chiefly mountainous, with the highest elevations in the Pamir and Alai ranges in the southeast; lower elevations in the northwest, southwest, and Fergana Valley in the far north. Mountains contain dense river networks and numerous glaciers. Lakes are primarily in the Pamir region in the east.

Rivers: Surkhob, Bartang, and Murgab

Climate: Mainly continental, with vast differences according to elevation. Highest temperatures are in the arid subtropical lowlands in the southwest; lowest temperatures are at the highest altitudes. Lowest precipitation is in the eastern Pamirs; highest precipitation near Fedchenko Glacier.

Government

Capital: Dushanbe

Date of independence: September 9, 1991

Government type: Republic

President: Imomali Rakhmonov

People

Population: 6,020,095 (1998)

Ethnic groups: Tajik, 64.9 percent; Uzbek, 25 percent; Russian, 3.5 percent; other, 6.6 percent

Official languages: Tajik, Russian

Religions: Sunni Muslim, 90 percent

Economy

Monetary unit: ruble

Exchange rate: 1,357.14 = US $1 (Oct. 1999)

Labor force: Agriculture and forestry, 52 percent; services, 31 percent; manufacturing, mining, and construction, 17 percent

Gross domestic product per capita: $700

TURKMENISTAN

Geography

Area: 188,456 square miles

Topography: Dominated by Turan Depression and Kara-Kum Desert; flatlands cover nearly 80 percent of the country. Elevation reaches 9,554 feet in the Kopet-Dag range along the southwestern border. Balkan Mountains are in the far west and Kugitang range in the far east.

Rivers: Amu, Murgab, and Tedzhen

Climate: Continental, subtropical, and desert with little rainfall; heaviest precipitation in the Kopet-Dag range.

Government

Capital: Ashkhabad

Date of independence: October 27, 1991

Government type: Republic

President: Saparmurat Niyazov

People

Population: 4,297,629 (1998)

Ethnic groups: Turkmen, 77 percent; Uzbek, 9.2 percent; Russian, 6.7 percent; Kazakh, 2 percent

Official languages: Turkmen, English, Russian

Religions: Sunni Muslim, 89 percent; Russian Orthodox, 9 percent

Economy

Monetary unit: manat

Exchange rate: 7,600 = US $1 (Aug. 1999)

Labor force: Agriculture and forestry, 44 percent; industry and construction, 19 percent

Gross domestic product per capita: $3,000

UZBEKISTAN

Geography

Area: 172,741 square miles

Topography: About 80 percent is flat desert; mountain ranges in the far southeast and far northeast. The Fergana Valley in the northeast is the most fertile region. There are few lakes and rivers. The Aral Sea is shared with Kazakhstan. Most of the country is seismically active.

Rivers: Amu, Zeravshan

Climate: Continental with sparse rainfall in most regions

Government

Capital: Tashkent

Date of independence: August 31, 1991

Government type: Republic

President: Islam A. Karimov

People

Population: 23,784,321 (1998)

Ethnic groups: Uzbek, 80 percent; Russian, 5.5 percent; Tajik, 5 percent; Kazakh, 3 percent; Karakalpak, 2.5 percent; Tatar, 1.5 percent

Official languages: Uzbek, Russian

Religions: Sunni Muslim, 88 percent; Russian Orthodox, 9 percent

Economy

Monetary unit: som

Exchange rate: 787.56 = US $1 (Oct. 2000)

Labor force: Agriculture and forestry, 44 percent; industry and construction, 20 percent

Gross domestic product per capita: $2,500

NOTES

CHAPTER 1: THE LAND AND PEOPLE

1. Gregory Gleason, *The Central Asian States: Discovering Independence.* Boulder, CO: Westview Press, 1997, p. 26.

CHAPTER 2: FROM THE SILK ROAD TO THE FALL OF THE SOVIET UNION

2. Quoted in Owen Lattimore and Eleanor Lattimore, *Silks, Spices, and Empire: Asia Seen Through the Eyes of Its Discoverers.* New York: Delacorte Press, 1968, pp. 28–29.

3. Quoted in Lattimore and Lattimore, *Silks, Spices, and Empire*, p. 114.

4. Quoted in Irene M. Franck and David M. Brownstone, *The Silk Road: A History.* New York: Facts On File, 1986, p. 246.

CHAPTER 3: THE INDEPENDENT STATES OF CENTRAL ASIA

5. Gleason, *The Central Asian States*, p. 13.

6. Askar Akayev, "Diplomacy of the Silk Road." www. Kyrgyzstan.org.

7. Gleason, *The Central Asian States*, p. 17.

8. Joseph Fritchett, "A Resurgent Russian Influence Grips Former Soviet Central Asia," *International Herald Tribune*, August 9, 2000.

9. Gleason, *The Central Asian States*, p. 18.

10. Eugene Romer, "Fear and Loathing in the 'Stans,'" *Christian Science Monitor*, August 8, 2000, p. 11.

CHAPTER 4: DAILY LIFE IN CENTRAL ASIA

11. Bradley Mayhew, Richard Plunkett, Simon Richmond, John King, John Noble, and Andrew Humphreys, *Central Asia.* Oakland, CA: Lonely Planet, 2000, p. 117.

12. Glenn E. Curtis, ed., *Kazakstan, Kyrgyzstan, Tajikistan,*

Turkmenistan, and Uzbekistan: Country Studies. Washington, DC: Library of Congress, 1997, p. 231.

13. Jonathon Maslow, *Sacred Horses: The Memoirs of a Turkmen Cowboy.* New York: Random House, 1994, p. 36.

14. Mayhew et al., *Central Asia,* p. 472.

15. Mayhew et al., *Central Asia,* p. 49.

16. Mayhew et al., *Central Asia,* p. 160.

17. Curtis, *Kazakstan, Kyrgyzstan, Tajikistan, Turkmenistan, and Uzbekistan,* p. 349.

18. Mayhew et al., *Central Asia,* p. 158.

19. Curtis, *Kazakstan, Kyrgyzstan, Tajikistan, Turkmenistan, and Uzbekistan,* p. 40.

20. Mayhew et al., *Central Asia,* p. 139.

CHAPTER 5: A RICH CULTURAL TAPESTRY

21. Edgar Knobloch, *Beyond the Oxus: Archaeology, Art, and Architecture of Central Asia.* London: Ernest Benn, 1972, p. 51.

22. Mayhew et al., *Central Asia,* p. 16.

23. Knobloch, *Beyond the Oxus,* p. 55.

24. Knobloch, *Beyond the Oxus,* p. 129.

25. Quoted in "The Kazak Film Industry: Reeling," *Economist,* February 5, 2000.

CHAPTER 6: CONFLICT AND COOPERATION ALONG THE NEW SILK ROAD

26. Rachel Denber, "Central Asia and the Caucasus Repeat Past Mistakes on Human Rights," *Eurasia Insight,* June 21, 2000. www.Eurasianet.org.

27. Bea Hogan, "Internet Latest Battleground to Control Central Asia," *Central Asia-Caucasus Analyst,* July 19, 2000. www.cacianalyst.org.

28. Akayev, "Diplomacy of the Silk Road."

29. Maria Utyaganova, "Kyrgyzstan's Kumtor Gold: Is It Worth the Environmental Risk?" *Central Asia-Caucasus Analyst,* July 5, 2000. www.cacianalyst.org.

30. Kunduz Sydygaliova, "Lesson of Batken," *Central Asia-Caucasus Analyst,* June 7, 2000. www.cacianalyst.org.

31. Quoted in Michael Madon, "Uzbekistan's Military Doctrine Is Tested by Insurgents," *Eurasia Insight*, August 8, 2000. www.Eurasianet.org.

32. Fritchett, "Resurgent Russian Influence."

33. Fritchett, "Resurgent Russian Influence."

34. Erika Dailey, "New USAID Strategy for Central Asia Reveals Disappointment in Democratic Reform," *Eurasia Insight*, September 21, 2000. www.Eurasianet.org.

CHRONOLOGY

B.C.

530–330
Achaemenid Empire in Central Asia consists of Sogdiana, Khorezm, and Saka.

329–327
Alexander the Great conquers most of Central Asia.

128
Chang Ch'ien visits Bactria; trade along Silk Road increases.

A.D.

ca. 450
Huns in control of Central Asia.

559
Turks drive the Huns out of Central Asia.

642
Muslim armies cross the Syr River and take Merv.

751
Arabs, Turks, and Tibetans defeat the Chinese at the Battle of the Talas River; the Chinese are driven out of Central Asia; the Muslim conquest of Central Asia is complete.

ca. 800
Islam becomes the dominant religion in Central Asia.

990s
Seljuq Empire is founded in Iran and part of present-day Turkmenistan.

999
Karakhanids overthrow Sāmānids and gain control of eastern Central Asia.

1130s
Karakitays conquer the Karakhanids and dominate Central Asia for one hundred years.

1150s
Khorezmshahs gain control of southern and eastern Central Asia and remain in power until the early thirteenth century.

1218–1295
Mongols conquer Central Asia, reducing Iranian influence and destroying cultural centers.

1350s–1750s
A succession of warring clans, including the Turkmen, Uzbeks, Kazakhs, and Zhungarians, seek control of Central Asia.

1380–1405
Timur the Lame (Tamerlane) unifies Mongol holdings in Central Asia and establishes capital at Samarqand.

1726
Kazakhs seek Russian protection from invaders, beginning the Russian annexation of the region.

1785–1820s
British and Russians begin rivalry for territory; Russians colonize Central Asia.

1885
All of Central Asia is under Russian control.

1914
Outbreak of World War I.

1916
Kazakh, Kyrgyz, Turkmen, and Uzbek uprisings in Central Asia against Russian conscription and land confiscation are met by bloody reprisals; thousands are massacred and many Kazakhs and Kyrgyz flee to China.

1917
Russian Revolution brings Bolsheviks to power; creation of the Soviet Union.

1918
World War I ends.

1918–1919
Widespread famine in Central Asia.

mid–1920s
Central Asia is under Soviet rule; Soviets redraw borders to create the current boundaries of Kazakhstan, Kyrgyzstan, Tajikistan, Turkmenistan, and Uzbekistan.

1927–1934
Waves of Communist Party purges in Central Asia; forced collectivization leads to widespread famine.

1939
World War II begins.

1941–1943
Many Soviet factories and plants are relocated to Central Asia to avoid capture by invading Nazis.

1945
World War II ends.

1956–1964
A second wave of Communist purges sweeps Central Asia.

1985
Mikhail Gorbachev is elected the first secretary of the Communist Party of the Soviet Union and institutes reform programs.

1987–1990
Political opposition groups form; demonstrations, protests, and riots begin in Central Asia.

1991
In August an attempted coup against Gorbachev fails, and Uzbekistan and Kyrgyzstan declare independence from the USSR; Tajikistan declares independence in September; Turkmenistan declares independence in October; Kazakhstan declares independence in December; the five Central Asian States sign the Alma-Ata Declaration formally establishing the Commonwealth of Independent States (CIS) on December 21.

1992
The five Central Asian States join the Economic Cooperation Organization (ECO); civil war begins in Tajikistan.

1993
Kazakhstan, Kyrgyzstan, Tajikistan, and Uzbekistan join five other CIS states, including Russia, in an economic union.

1994

Kazakhstan, Kyrgyzstan, Turkmenistan, and Uzbekistan join the North Atlantic Treaty Organization (NATO).

1995

Kazakhstan and Kyrgyzstan sign a ten-year partnership and cooperation agreement with the European Union (EU).

1997

June peace accord formally ends the civil war in Tajikistan.

SUGGESTIONS FOR FURTHER READING

BOOKS

Aleksandr Belenitsky, *Central Asia*. New York: New World, 1968. This book examines Central Asian archaeological remains from the Paleolithic Period through the Arab conquest.

John Channon and Robert Hudson, *The Penguin Historical Atlas of Russia*. New York: Penguin, 1995. Useful historical and geographical information on Russia both before and after the fall of the Soviet Union.

Mohammad-Reza Djalili, Frédéric Grare, and Shirin Akiner, eds., *Tajikistan: The Trials of Independence*. New York: St. Martin's Press, 1997. This book examines the civil war and other difficulties faced by Tajikistan in its first years of independence.

Mehrdad Haghayeghi, *Islam and Politics in Central Asia*. New York: St. Martin's Press, 1995.

Islam Karimov, *Uzbekistan on the Threshold of the Twenty-First Century: Challenges to Stability and Progress*. New York: St. Martin's Press, 1998. Written by the current president of Uzbekistan, this account of the Uzbek political situation is nevertheless informative.

Martha Brill Olcott, *The Kazakhs*. 2nd ed. Stanford, CA: Hoover Institution Press, 1995. Written by a leading authority on Central Asia, this book provides an in-depth look at the Kazakh people.

WEBSITES

Central Asia-Caucasus Analyst (www.cacianalyst.org). This site covers all of the recently independent states in Central Asia and the Caucasus, with an emphasis on the analysis of developments in the region by Western scholars and other experts.

Eurasia Insight (www.Eurasianet.org). The reporting on this site relies on journalists from Central Asia and neighboring countries and on reporters based in the United States. It includes sections on human rights, the environment, and elections and has links to other resources on Central Asia.

WORKS CONSULTED

BOOKS

Glenn E. Curtis, ed., *Kazakstan, Kyrgyzstan, Tajikistan, Turkmenistan, and Uzbekistan: Country Studies.* Washington, DC: Library of Congress, 1997. This book profiles the history, culture, politics, economy, and environment of the five Central Asian States.

Irene M. Franck and David M. Brownstone, *The Silk Road: A History.* New York: Facts On File, 1986. This history of the Silk Road contains quotations from numerous historic figures such as Ptolemy and Marco Polo.

Gregory Gleason, *The Central Asian States: Discovering Independence.* Boulder, CO: Westview Press, 1997. The author traces events in Central Asia from the Soviet era through the breakup of the USSR and independence for the five republics.

Johannes Kalter and Margareta Pavaloi, eds., *Uzbekistan: Heirs to the Silk Road.* London: Thames and Hudson, 1997. This art history book contains numerous color photographs of relics found in Uzbekistan.

Edgar Knobloch, *Beyond the Oxus: Archaeology, Art, and Architecture of Central Asia.* London: Ernest Benn, 1972. This comprehensive guide to Central Asia contains numerous photographs of the region's artifacts, some of which date back to before the common era.

Manuel Komroff, ed., *The Travels of Marco Polo.* New York: Modern Library, 1953. After his return to Venice in 1295 from a twenty-six-year visit to the court of Kublai Khan in China, Marco Polo wrote his experiences in this famous travel guide that has remained popular throughout the centuries.

Luc Kwanten, *Imperial Nomads: A History of Central Asia, 500–1500.* Philadelphia: University of Pennsylvania Press, 1979. This book contains an in-depth history of Central Asia from just before the rise of Islam through the Mongol era.

Owen Lattimore and Eleanor Lattimore, *Silks, Spices, and Empire: Asia Seen Through the Eyes of Its Discoverers.* New York: Delacorte Press, 1968. This book contains annotated excerpts from journals of historical travelers to the region.

Jonathon Maslow, S*acred Horses: The Memoirs of a Turkmen Cowboy.* New York: Random House, 1994. Maslow, an American writer, went to Turkmenistan at the end of the Soviet era to learn about the legendary Akal Teke horses.

Bradley Mayhew, Richard Plunkett, Simon Richmond, John King, John Noble, and Andrew Humphreys, *Central Asia.* Oakland, CA: Lonely Planet, 2000. This travel guide contains informative sections on such topics as the history, geography, climate, environment, politics, and economy of Central Asia.

Susan Whitfield, *Life Along the Silk Road.* Berkeley and Los Angeles: University of California Press, 1999. Covering life along the Silk Road at different times from the years 750 to 1000, this book offers an interesting glimpse into the people, culture, and history of the region.

Michael Wood, *In the Footsteps of Alexander the Great: A Journey from Greece to Asia.* Berkeley and Los Angeles: University of California Press, 1997. This book, which contains numerous maps and color photographs, was published to accompany the BBC television series of the same title.

PERIODICALS

Joseph Fritchett, "A Resurgent Russian Influence Grips Former Soviet Central Asia," *International Herald Tribune,* August 9, 2000.

"The Kazak Film Industry: Reeling," *Economist,* February 5, 2000.

Eugene Romer, "Fear and Loathing in the 'Stans,'" *Christian Science Monitor,* August 8, 2000.

INTERNET SOURCES

Askar Akayev, "Diplomacy of the Silk Road." www.Kyrgyzstan.org.

Chris Aslan, "Military Music Videos as Uzbek Pop Propaganda," *Central Asia-Caucasus Analyst*, July 30, 2000. www.cacianalyst.org.

Erika Dailey, "New USAID Strategy for Central Asia Reveals Disappointment in Democratic Reform," *Eurasia Insight*, September 21, 2000. www.Eurasianet.org.

Rachel Denber, "Central Asia and the Caucasus Repeat Past Mistakes on Human Rights," *Eurasia Insight*, June 21, 2000. www.Eurasianet.org.

Bea Hogan, "Internet Latest Battleground to Control Central Asia," *Central Asia-Caucasus Analyst*, July 19, 2000. www.cacianalyst.org.

Michael Madon, "Uzbekistan's Military Doctrine Is Tested by Insurgents," *Eurasia Insight*, August 8, 2000. www.Eurasianet.org.

"Press Freedom Suffers During Kyrgyzstan's Presidential Campaign," *Eurasia Insight*, October 12, 2000. www.Eurasianet.org.

Kunduz Sydygaliova, "Lesson of Batken," *Central Asia-Caucasus Analyst*, June 7, 2000. www.cacianalyst.org.

Maria Utyaganova, "Kyrgyzstan's Kumtor Gold: Is It Worth the Environmental Risk?" *Central Asia-Caucasus Analyst*, July 5, 2000. www.cacianalyst.org.

INDEX

Abay (movie), 88
Achaemenid Empire (Iran), 29, 77
Afghanistan, 30, 105
  drugs and, 41, 100, 102
  Russian troops and, 103–104
agriculture
  cities and, 21
  collectivized by Soviets, 36
  cotton and silk processing, 22
  economy and, 92
  Fergana Valley and, 18
  land and water management, 43
  mountain ranges and, 13
  pollution and, 17
  soil infertility and, 98
Aitmatov, Chinghis, 85
Akayev, Askar, 46–49, 59
  on economic development, 95
ak kalpak (hat), 64
akyn (storytellers), 85
Alai (mountain range), 11–12
Albright, Madeline, 102
Alexander the Great, 9, 26
  conquest of Central Asia by, 30
  Samarqand and, 20
Almaty (Kazakhstan), 22, 66
Alpamish (Uzbek epic), 85
Altay Shan (mountain range), 10, 12
Amu River (Amu Dar'ya), 17, 69
Aqtaū (city), 68
  bubonic plague and, 73
Arabs, 9, 30
  music and, 86
  suppression of traditional art by, 79
Aral Sea, 10–11
  conflicts over water and, 95
  pollution in, 18
  river flowing into, 17
  shrinking of, 18, 20
  Soviets and, 38
architecture, 80–82
Arch of Neutrality, 23
art, 77–79
  Ngan-yang, China and, 77
  plant and animal designs in, 83
Artush (Kygyzstan), 14
aryan (beverage), 63
Ashkhabad (Turkmenistan)
  bazaars in, 65
  earthquake in, 13–14, 22
  weather and, 16
Assyrians, 77
Azerbaijan, 93

Bactria, 30
Bakhara (city), 29, 33
Battle of the Talas River, 31

Baykonur Cosmodrome (Kazakhstan), 94
besbarmak (food), 62
Besh Kumpyr (*Five Old Ladies*, film), 88
Bishkek (Kyrgyzstan), 22, 66
Bolo-hauz (mosque), 80
Bolshevik Russia, 35
  destruction of buildings by, 80
Britain. *See* Great Britain
Buddhism, 29
  influence on art, 77, 78
Bukhara (Uzbekistan), 20–21, 27, 69

Caspian Sea, 10–11
  flooding and, 18
  oil wastes and, 98
  ports at, 68
Central Asia
  ancestors of, 7
  China, relations with, 53, 55, 89–90
  clothing of, 64–65
  five independent nations of, 10–11, 39
  food of, 54, 62–63
  geography of, 10–23, 26
  infrastructure of, 45
  invasions and, 26
  Iran, relations with, 55
  nationalism and, 40, 49–50, 52
  nuclear weapons, 38, 52–53
  resources requisitioned by Russia, 35
  Russian immigrants and, 34–35, 50–51
  Russian relations and, 103
  during World War II, 37
Chang Ch'ien, 26
Chärjew (Turkmenistan), 69
China, 7
  as conquerors, 30
  food from, 62
  goods sent from, 28
  influence on culture by, 77
  Mongols and, 33
  relations with, 53, 55, 105
  Silk Road and, 8, 27–28
  Xinjiang province and, 89
Chu (River), 18, 22
climate, 19
  cities and, 20
  desertification, 16–17
  drought and, 97
  flooding and, 18
  pollution effect on, 95–96
Commonwealth of Independent States
  (CIS), 41, 51–52
Communism Peak (mountain), 13
Communist Revolution, 9
conflicts, 7
  water and, 43, 95
Cossacks, 24

cotton, 18, 34
  the economy and, 92
  irrigation of and environment, 20
  processing of, 22
  U.S. Civil War and, 34
  water and, 96
culture, 77–88
  conquests, effect on, 9
  of contrasts, 56
  diversity of, 7–8
  Greeks and, 30
  holidays, festivals and, 73–74
  promotion of local, 49
  Silk Road and, 29
  tea ceremony and, 54
  traditions of gender roles, 57
  yurts, importance of in, 62

dabyl (percussion instrument), 86
dauylpaz (percussion instrument), 86
decolonization, 43–45
defense, 52–53, 55
dombra (stringed instrument), 85, 86
doppe (skullcap), 64
drugs
  Afghanistan and, 41, 100, 102
  relations with China and, 55
  Russian troops and, 104
Dushanbe (Tajikistan), 22
  mudslide and earthquake in, 15
  shopping in, 66
Dushanbe Declaration, 90
dutar (stringed instrument), 86

earthquakes, 13–15
economics, 9
  commerce, centers of, 22
  cooperation and, 51
  corruption and, 46
  currency and, 51–52
  environmental disasters and, 51
  global economy and, 92
  oil and gas reserves, 93
  Russian assistance with, 103
  Silk Road and, 26, 29
  stagnation of, 55
  Uzbeks and, 46
  wages and work situations, 66–67
  Western investments and, 93, 95
ecosystems, 12–13
  deserts, 10, 15–17
  evergreen forests, 13
  lakes and seas, 18–19
  mountains, 12
  pamir (pasture), 13
  pollution and, 18
  rivers, 17
  steppe, 10
education
  compulsory nature of, 57, 60
  madrasahs (Islamic universities), 57
  problems with, 70–71
  university degree programs in, 71
Eid-ul-Azha (Feast of Sacrifice), 74
Eid-ul-Fitr (Islamic holy day), 74
elechek (women's turban), 65
emir of Bukhara, 21
environmental concerns

agriculture and, 98
Aral Sea Basin and, 95
natural resources and, 98–100
nuclear weapons testing and, 38
soft laws and, 99–100
Er Sain (Kazakhstan oral history), 85
Er Targyn (Kazakhstan oral history), 85
European Union, 41
  euro, 51
ethnic groups, 7
  civil unrest and, 22
  conflicts, obstacles to progress, 89
  division of by Soviets, 35
  economic reform and, 43
  five main groups of, 23
  immigrants as, 24–25
  independence, effects on, 40
  minority rights and, 49–50
  Russians as, 51
Eurasia Film Festival (Kazakhstan), 87

Fan Mountains, 22
Fedchenko Glacier (Tajikistan), 13
Feraghy, Magtumguly, 85
Fergana Valley, 11, 17–18
  agriculture and, 11
  ethnic groups in, 50
  horses in, 26
  land and water disputes in, 43
  Silk Road and, 27
folk art, 82–85
foreign relations, 89–90

Gagarin, Yury, 94
Genghis Khan, 32, 82
  destruction of buildings by, 80
Ghaznavid (dynasty), 32
Gorno-Badakhshan region (Tajikistan), 22
  drug traffic through, 102
government
  effect on economics, 52
  instability of, 55
  Internet and, 90–92
  leadership vacuum and, 43, 45
  political repression and, 47–49, 89–92,
    101
  Soviets and, 9, 36
  unilatereteral systems of, 90
  water use and, 96–97
  women in, 56–59
Great Britain, 9
  expansion to India by, 34
Great Game, 9
Great Uzbek Highway, 69
Greek Civil War, 25
Greeks, 7
  art and, 77
  influence of, 30–31, 78
  in Uzbekistan, 24–25
GUM (department store), 66
Gur Emir Mausoleum, 34, 81–82
Gurogly (Turkmen epic), 85

halal, 62
Hans, 26
health care, 72–73
  environment and, 73
Hojent (Tajikistan), 30

horses, 26
  depicted in art, 83
  for recreation, 74–76
  Turkmenistan and, 44
housing, 60–62
human rights, 90, 105
Human Rights Watch, 90
Huns, 30–31
Hurakan (hurricane), 16

ikat (cloth), 65
Ili River (Kazakhstan), 19, 22
India, 7, 9
  architecture and, 80
  conquests by, 30
  food from, 62
  goods sent from, 28
  influence on art, 78
  influence on culture, 77
  Kushans and, 31
  Russian policy and, 34
  Silk Road and, 27–28
International League for Human Rights, 90
International Monetary Fund, 46
Iran
  art and, 77
  food from, 11, 24, 62, 105
  Iranian Parthians, 31
  oil and gas reserves and, 93
  political influence of, 89
  Silk Road and, 27–28
  Soviet nuclear weapons and, 53
Iraq, 53, 80
Irtysh River, 13, 68
Islam, 7, 24, 29
  in China, 89–90
  food forbidden by, 52
  Kazakhstan and, 73
  Muslim fundamentalists and, 41
  reasons for conversions, 31–32
  repression by Soviets, 36–37
islimi (floral art motifs), 79
Ismail Samani Mausoleum (Bukhara), 82
iwan (arched portal), 81

Judaism, 25, 29, 42
Juma Mosque (Khiva), 80

Kabul (Afghanistan), 100
Kaifeng (China), 27
Kajik Soviet Socialist Republic (USSR), 22
Kalon Minaret (Bukhara), 80
Karakalpak Autonomous Republic (USSR), 7–8, 24
Karakalpakstan, 24
Karakhanid (dynasty), 32
Karakitay (dynasty), 32
Kara-Kum Canal, 20
Kara-Kum Desert (black sands), 11, 15
  climate of, 19
  Turkmen and, 24
Karimov, Islam, 105
Karlovy Vary Film Festival, 88
Kashgar (China), 27
Kazakh, 7
  bubonic plague and, 73
  language and, 23
Kazakhstan, 10

film industry in, 88
the Internet and, 92
market reform in, 93
nuclear weapons and, 52–53
oil and gas reserves and, 93
Russian influence on, 10
transportation and, 67–68
khalem (food), 73
Khorezm, 29
Khorezmshah (dynasty), 32
Khudzhand (city), 32
kiyiz, 60
Koblandy-batir (Kazakhstan oral history), 85
kobyz (stringed instrument), 86
Kokand (city), 27
Kopet-Dag (mountain range), 11
Koreans, 22, 25
Korkut Ata (Turkman epic), 85
Kufic (script), 79
Kulov, Felix, 47–49, 90
kumys (beverage), 63
  folk art and, 83
Kunabaev, Abay, 85
Kurds, 25
Kushan Empire, 30–31
  art and, 78
Kymyzuryndyk (Islamic festival), 73
Kyrgyz, 7, 79
  nomadic herders, 23
Kyrgyz Academy of Sciences, 46
Kyrgyzstan, 10–11
  gas shortages and, 68
  independence and, 40
  political repression and, 90
  role of women in, 58–59
  traditional clothing of, 65
Kyzyl-Kum Desert (red sands), 11, 15, 17

laghman (food), 62
Lake Balkhash (Kazakhstan), 19
Lake Issyk-Kul (Kyrgyzstan), 18, 100
language
  alphabets and, 38, 70, 91
  elections and, 49
  English as language of business, 7
  invasions and, 26
  Iranian, 9, 29
  roots of, 23–24
  promotion of local, 49
  Soviet colonialism and, 7, 35
literature, 85–86
Lost Love of Genghis Khan; Shankhai (movie), 88

Macedon, 30
madrasahs (Islamic colleges)
  architecture of, 80–81
Manas (epic poem), 79, 85
Manichaeism, 29, 78
manpar (food), 62
manty (food), 62–63
Mawlid-an-Nabi (Islamic holy day), 74
Mecca (Saudi Arabia), 31
Mediterranean Sea, 27, 62
Merv (Turkmenistan)
  Mongols and, 33
  Muslim city of, 21

Silk Road and, 20, 27
Turks defeated in, 31
Middle East
  food from, 62
  Mongols and, 33
mihrab (mosque architecture), 80
Mongolian Empire, 9, 32–33
  art and, 77
  capitol of, 21
  influence on language, 23
  Merv destroyed by, 21
  Uzbeks, decendants of, 24
movies, 87–88
Muhammad, 31
Museum of Applied Arts (Tashkent), 84–85
music, 86–87
  military propaganda and, 86
  modern, 87

nan (food), 63
Naryn River, 17
national defense, 52–53, 55
natural resources, 34
  copper, 19
  gold, 18, 100
  oil and gas, 18
  Russian exploitation of, 34
  United States and, 104
Navrus (Islamic holiday), 73
Nazarbayev, Nursultan, 93
nishalda (food), 63
Niyazov, Saparmurat, 22–23, 41, 105
  and economics, 93

Ob' (River), 13
oil and gas
  pollution and, 18
  Soviets and, 93
  United States assistance with, 104
Otyrar (Kazakhstan), 32

Pamir (mountain range), 11–12
  Amu River, source waters in, 17
  as natural barrier, 22
  Silk Road and, 27
Persia, 9, 7
  art and, 77
  craftsmen and, 80
  influence on culture, 77
  literature and, 85
  Tajiks and, 24
Petropavlovsk (city), 100
piala (tea cup), 54
piroshki (food), 63
Plesetsk Cosmodrome (Russia), 94
plov (food), 62
Pobeda Peak, 13
pollution
  agriculture and, 17
  copper mining and, 19
  environmental disasters and, 100
  health care and, 73
  nuclear waste as, 38
  oil and natural gas and, 18
population
  ethnic groups in, 22
  largest area of, 18
  Silk Road and, 20

water and, 20
Putin, Vladimir, 103

Qŭqon (Uzbekistan), 69
  sacked by Russia, 35
Qur'an (Koran), 31
Qyzylorda, 73

rabab (stringed instrument), 86
Ramadan, 74
religion
  repression of, by Soviets, 36
  invasions and, 26
  Silk Road and, 29
Res Publica (Public Affairs), 47, 101
Rubáiyát of Omar Kayyám, The
  (Khayyam), 85
Rūdaki, Abū 'Abdollāh (poet), 85
Russia, 24
  capital investment and, 93
  Central Asian defense and, 52
  colonialism of, 23, 33–35
  food from, 62
  goods sent to China by, 28
  influence of, 89
  Kazakhstan and, 10
  Mongols and, 7, 22, 33, 55, 105
  rocket testing and, 94
  Russian Empire, 9, 34
  Russian Revolution and, 35
  technological advances of, 35

Sakas (kingdom), 20, 29–30
Sāmānid (dynasty), 32, 85
Samaritans, 77
Samarqand (Uzbekistan), 27, 32, 69
  architecture in, 80
  as bartering center, 29
  Mongols and, 33
  railroad and, 69
  in seventh century, 32
  shopping in, 66
  Silk Road and, 27
Sassanids, 30–31
Scythians, 77
Seljuq Empire, 24, 32
Semey Nuclear Testing Site (Kazakhstan),
  38
Semipalatinsky (Kazakhstan)
  nuclear weapons facility, 52–53
Setora (singing group), 86
shanrak (yurt architecture), 60
shashlyk (food), 62
Shaybanid khanate, 21
Sher Dor, 81
Shinarbayev, Yermek, 88
shopping, 65–66
shorpa (food), 62
shubat (beverage), 63
shyrdaks (rugs), 60, 84
Silk Road, 7, 8–9, 26–29
  effect of ocean routes on, 29
  population effects on, 20
Sogdiana (kingdom), 29, 30, 31
  art and, 78
Soviet era, 9, 35–38
  break up of, 38–39
  colonialism and, 7

Dushanbe and rail line and, 22
glasnost, perestroika and, 38
horse training, effect on, 44
mismanagement of land and resources by, 38
movies and, 87
national identities and, 7
nationalism, fear of, 35
nuclear testing, 38
political repression by, 36
positive influences of, 38
sozanda (folk music), 87
sports and recreation, 74–76
Stalin, Joseph, 36
Sultan Sanjar Mausoleum (Merv), 82
sumalakh (food), 73
suzani (silk coverlets), 84
sybyzgy (wind instrument), 86
Syr River (Syr Dar'ya), 17
navigation on, 68

Tajik, 7, 23
music and, 87
traditional clothing of, 65
Tajikistan, 10
civil war in, 41
Persian inhabitants, 24
political repression and, 90
Russian troops in, 104
transportation in, 68
Taklimakan Desert (China), 27
takyr (cracked clay), 15
tapan (coat), 65
Tashkent (Uzbekistan), 20, 27, 69
agricultural community, 21–22
earthquake in, 14
ethnic population of, 22
Tashkent Spice Girls. *See* Setora
Tatars, 22–24
Crimean Tatars, 25
influence on language, 32
Russian Tatars, 33
telpek (hat), 64
Termiz (Uzbekistan), 69
Mongols and, 33
terrorism
drugs in financing of, 102
nuclear weapons and, 53
relations with China and, 55
Tian Shan (mountain range), 10–12, 27
Timur's tomb, 33
Timur the Lame (Tamerlane), 34
architecture and, 80
rebuilding of Samarqand by, 33
tizgych (yurt architecture), 60
Tolkuchka Bazaar (Turkmenistan), 65
topography
glaciers, 13
mountains, 12–13
Tosh Khovli Palace, 82
Transcaspian Railroad, 69
Transoxiana, 31
transportation, 67–70
obstacle to progress of, 89
TsUM (department store), 66
Turan Depression, 11
Turkey, 41

oil and gas reserves and, 93
political influence of, 89
Turkic,
languages derived from, 7
Turkmen, 7, 23
as nomadic horse breeders, 24
traditional clothing of, 65
Turkmenbashi (Turkmenistan), 23, 69
Turkmenistan, 10–11
independence and, 41
the Internet and, 92
music and, 87
oil and gas reserves and, 93
political repression and, 90
separation of sexes in, 59
transportation in, 68–69
Turks, 30, 31
tus-kiiz (wall carpet), 84

Ukraine, 24
United States
capital investment and, 93
military assistance by, 104
political influence of, 89
Univermag (department store), 66
Ural Mountains, 10
Urugan (evil spirit), 16
U.S. Agency for International Development (USAID), 105
Utyaganova, Maria
Islam and, 46
on mining, 99–100
Uzbek, 7, 23
music and, 87
traditional clothing of, 65
Uzbekistan, 7, 10–11
Caucasians in, 22
climate of, 20
cotton and, 4
Greeks in, 24
independence and, 40–41
political repression and, 90
tomb of Alexander the Great in, 30
transportation and, 69–70
women's savings parties in, 59
Uzbek Soviet Socialist Republic (USSR), 21

women, 56–59
economics and, 59
education and, 57
music and, 87
as second class citizens, 57–59
sex-role customs and, 56–57
violence and, 58

Xuanzang, 32

Yalla (music group), 87
yurts, 9, 62
Yuzhnyy Airport (Uzbekistan), 70

Zarafshon Highway, 69
zhetigen (stringed instrument), 86
Zoroastrianism, 29
and art, 78
symbols on mausoleums, 82
Zvezda (space station module), 94

Picture Credits

About the Authors

Cherese Cartlidge and Charles Clark are freelance writers and editors who live in Georgia. Cherese attended New Mexico State University, where she received a B.A. in psychology. Charles attended New Mexico Highlands University and received degrees in philosophy and psychology. He and Cherese have been collaborating on writing and editing projects since 1998.